'Just fabulous. A close-up, be[z] life as it is really lived, through all, love. Dianne is a poet and beautiful. While telling of their his journey through his gamb. opening story which spares nothing and ends with great positivity as Tony goes on to help other gamblers. I keenly felt Dianne's innate love of people and her creativity in art, her nurturing of extended family and many friendships – and her devastating loss when Tony dies. And even then, there is beauty and hope. A truly moving book.'

Frances Liardet, author of *We Must Be Brave* and *Think of Me*

'Fascinating. Style is light and easy to read.'

Brian O'Reilly, former headteacher

Flutter is a memoir of a life well-lived and a recovery journey that touched many hearts and minds. Dianne's tribute to her husband Tony, Gamblers Anonymous and the twelve-step recovery programme beautifully showcases the energy and warmth that must have radiated from her husband during his many years of dedicated service to his fellowship. I hope this story of how Tony and Dianne recovered from co-dependency and gambling addiction finds its way into the hands of the people who need it most.

I am deeply touched to realise that by writing it, Dianne is enabling Tony's legacy of service to his beloved fellowship to continue from beyond the grave. We twelve-steppers stand on the shoulders of giants who have gone before us, and we owe it to them to keep passing it on.

Flutter is a fitting tribute to the memory of Tony, the fellowship of Gamblers Anonymous and Gam-Anon and the power of the twelve-step programme. It is also an important piece of UK recovery history and especially the history of Gamblers Anonymous and Gam-Anon which ought to be preserved for posterity. I am grateful to Dianne for her service in writing it.'

Dr Samantha Duggan, Chair of the All Party Parliamentary Group on Twelve-Step Recovery from Addiction

'Read this if you've ever been involved with a gambler or need reassurance that addiction can be overcome. A passionate, honest account of compulsive gambling, addiction, and the redemptive power of love.'

Isobel, Gam-Anon member

'I can only say how much reading *Flutter* spoke to me. It sometimes brought me to tears. Pete was a fruit machine gambler, but the traits of lying and so on were just as prevalent. It's written in a way that's easy to read and will help people realize that gambling can be overcome by going to GA and Gam-Anon and that people can find a new life together with love.'

Jill C, Gam-Anon member

FLUTTER
FLUTTER
FLUTTER
FLUTTER
FLUTTER
FLUTTER
FLUTTER

To Michael -
thank you so
much for your
support! Hope you
enjoy it. Dianne! X

FLUTTER
FLUTTER
FLUTTER
FLUTTER
FLUTTER
FLUTTER
FLUTTER

DIANNE SANGSTER

FOR HIM, GAMBLING WAS MORE THAN A FLUTTER. IT STOLE HIS LIFE...

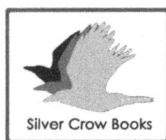

Silver Crow Books

Published under licence by Brown Dog Books, 10b Greenway Farm,
Bath Rd, Wick, nr. Bath BS30 5RL, UK

Supported by Silver Crow Books

ISBN printed book: 978-1-83952-916-0 (memoir)

Cover design by David Daniels
Internal design by Mac Style

Printed and bound in the UK

This book is printed on FSC® certified paper

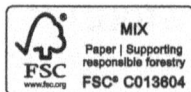

FSC

MIX
Paper | Supporting
responsible forestry
FSC® C013604

Tony

*I'd never set foot in a casino before. It was the epitome of glamour…
as soon as the croupier set the wheel spinning, the ball began to click
around and my gut started to churn – excitement needled up to my
scalp. The wheel slowed – the ball clattered and fell.*

Good God were those my *numbers?!*

Yes!

Maybe I could sort out my money worries…

I'd come home.

I never wanted to leave…

Contents

Tony died some time ago. I have recreated his voice, so that he can tell his own story.

Names are changed to protect people's privacy.

Prologue

Chiswick 2003

The wings of a pelican

Dianne

I had to hunt for the wings – couldn't remember where I'd stashed them. Our niece Rebecca wanted to photograph them for her Christmas card that year. Her photos were fab, like her Uncle Tony's.

Part of our large bedroom was my studio space, so I eventually looked under the bed – where they were, firmly wedged. I grasped their broom handle ends and wiggled. They slid out unscathed; except the black paint on the big cardboard feathers was grey – I've never been an enthusiastic duster.

I phoned her. 'Hi Becca, I found the pelican wings, do you fancy coming over this weekend?... Yep, we can play around with images... On the Green? Great idea. Tony might even bake us some bread.'

Our home was in Bedford Park, a second-floor mansion flat, with acres of carpet and light, rented from a friend living in New Zealand. It was our grandest temporary dwelling so far. Rebecca's eagle eye must have been honed partly from closely observing Tony's photographs. Above the mantelpiece in our living room was his large canvas close-up of the broken hinge of a playground gate bound together with blue rope. Nearby was the smaller image of a pure white hellebore with glass bubbles of dew, glowing from a bed of dark leaves. Taking up one whole wall in our kitchen was a montage of the skeleton of Brighton's West Pier, as it rusts away into the sea.

As Tony opened the oven door on the day of Rebecca's visit, we were blasted by a rush of hot baked bread and rosemary. He dragged out a tin of puffed gold. Focaccia – flecked with sea salt and chopped rosemary, drenched with olive oil. I found his version of traditional Ligurian bread even more delicious than any we'd tried on the Italian Riviera. My mouth was watering; I offered to do a quality check. He grinned, 'Still too hot! Let's wait till we're back from the park.'

I'd watch him leaning over the worktop, totally absorbed, flour everywhere, rocking with the rhythm of kneading the dough with his fists. In his usual single-minded way, he taught himself to be a fantastic baker – loads of research and endless trial and error – no giving up till it was perfect. He was considering starting a Saturday morning class in our expansive kitchen to teach others to bake his Fool-Proof-Multi-Bread.

His passions for baking and photography were about the only things that could lure him away from the computer and the phone. With his friend and business partner Bob, he ran a computer software company; but was semi-retired, and often worked from home. Whenever I got home from work at the Community Centre, I heard snatches of conversation on my way upstairs, which could be work-related, but were often from some brave soul taking the first step to stop his out-of-control gambling habit. Tony had been there himself, and for years had been a mentor for those struggling with addiction. This snippet was in response to a call for help: '... don't worry, we've all done terrible things; you'll find everyone's in the same boat ...' When I hello-hugged him, he turned around, adjusted his headphones to give me a quick kiss and a grin, then turned back to the screen to carry on talking and talking.

I'd got into art college as a mature student, with some expertise in making life sculptures from clay. At college, I enjoyed playing around with wire and papier mâché. For a postgraduate exhibition on identity, I made a larger-than-life sculpture of a pelican-woman, with human-ish breasts and arms modelled on mine, and called her *Rara avis*. Her ochre legs were thick as an elephant's, ending in great flat feet to ground her. She was a version of me as a mother, wife and Aussie expat. I had always loved the big black-and-white pelicans in Queensland, with their awkward shopping-bag-bills. I'd found a tale from the *Medieval Bestiary* in which a mother pelican becomes furiously impatient with her demanding chicks and kills them – by accident, one hopes – but is immediately remorseful, tearing at her breast, drawing blood to revive them, reminding me of times I had lost patience with my chicks – with less tragic results – usually ending in my apology. All that remained of *Rara avis* were the wings, as after the show I left her in the garden to disintegrate in the rain. But one very wet day I had second thoughts and scurried to save her detachable wings.

Becca turned up; after exchanging hugs we set off for the park with camera and wings, happy to have the focaccia to come back to. The Green was just over the road, edging Bedford Park, the first garden suburb in London. The triangle of Acton Green is bordered by generous old chestnuts and criss-crossed with paths, separated from Chiswick Common by the elevated District Line. Trains rattle above commuters on their way to and from Turnham Green station. Beech-brown leaves were scattered over the grass; a tang of loam was in the air. Our shadows were long. Gazing at the naked branches of a chestnut tracing dark lines over the gold of the lowering sun, I was reminded of church windows.

Tony and I started mucking about with the wings, much to the amusement of passers-by. 'Aunty Di, can you hold the wings *behind* Uncle?' Becca suggested. I gripped their wooden ends and hid from the camera, lining up the wings behind his outstretched arms. Tony tried to look angelic as Becca snapped away; he resembled Leonardo da Vinci's Vitruvian Man, with wings. My arms started feeling the weight of them, so I put them down. Then impetuously, I embraced Tony from behind – like one of those koala clips beloved of tourists leaving Brisbane airport – and snuggled into the familiar jumper-clad warmth of him. He held my arms close, and murmured over his shoulder, 'I love you, Dianne Elizabeth Sangster!'

Becca was using black-and-white film. She leaned the wings on a wooden bench with a gap in the middle, as if their owner had momentarily slipped away. With the scattering of leaves on the grass, and the path leading out of the frame, the monochrome image had a quiet poignancy. She later decided on that photograph for her card. She had also asked Tony to sit on the bench between the wings to take a few shots. In one resulting photo, he sits forward, relaxed. His hands dangle over the edge of the seat between his spread knees. One stout walking boot rests forward at an angle, the other's tucked under the bench. The white wings extending away from his black sweater appear as part of him. He has a fashionably short beard. His face gazes away from the camera and his glasses catch the sun. An aging, balding, strong-looking man; uncharacteristically not smiling, yet somehow loving. Our slightly wounded pelican angel.

Four years later we were to use that photo at his funeral.

PART ONE

Up to 1970s

Meeting, gambling, help

1

Queensland up to 1970 and getting to the UK

Dianne

L ong ago and far away I lived with my parents and sister Anna in a small town in Queensland about a hundred and sixty miles north of Brisbane. Maryborough had a timber mill which flooded frequently when the Mary River swelled as it snaked through the town, and an Italian milk bar that made creamy malted milks served in icy metal containers. Our mother worked for the Maryborough Chronicle as a journalist. When school finished, Anna would look after me until Mum got home. Dad was a commercial traveller then and was often away at work. Anna was older than me by six-and-a-half years and had more than the usual sisterly influence on my life. I looked up to her as if she were my mother, almost, and boy, it was a long way up! Even before she was a teenager this sister of mine showed every sign of great creativity and practical responsibility. She started entering competitions, eager to make a bit of pocket money. I remember the curly pink earrings she designed and made when she was about twelve, the first of her many wins. Like everyone else, I thought she was wonderful and clever and everything she did was laudable and proper. I adored her.

On the other hand, I would often perch up a tree reading for hours, which appeared to have no practical value. I developed a feeling of not being good enough. It wasn't sibling rivalry, as Anna never crowed about her achievements. It was just that she was already so accomplished. Throughout my childhood, this phrase echoed: 'Isn't Anna wonderful!' There was no hope of getting anywhere near her high bar. If my actual mother noticed me comparing myself unfavourably to my sister, she'd say, 'Just be yourself darling!' Good advice, but – what on earth was I? Still, I felt secure in the love of both our parents and am told I was a happy sunny child who smiled a lot at strangers.

Anna had piano lessons; I went to ballet classes. I have happy memories of all of us in the living room with Mother's beloved three-piece suite of Tasmanian myrtle, or silver beech. It was modern, covered with a dense leafy pattern resembling the designs of William Morris. The curved arms of the chairs gleamed, showing the wood's wiggly grain. In a dark wooden frame above the settee was a landscape of cattle meandering under gum trees at sunset.

Anna would play the piano with Father standing beside her singing in his delightful tenor voice, '… some enchanted evening – you may see a stranger – across a crowded room …' from Lerner and Loewe's *South Pacific*' (for instance); while Mum whistled tunefully – she had a brilliant whistle – and I danced about Artistically.

The women in my family were fashion-conscious. My mother was always stylish, and Anna became a superb seamstress who made many of her clothes almost as soon as she was old enough to thread a needle. When Mother eventually acquired her dream boutique, Anna designed and made clothes for it. As a teenager, I pored over copies of *Vogue* magazine, hopelessly outclassed by the glorious models, lusting after the clothes and envious of how they sat on those svelte women. In one edition, my eye was caught by a travel article about Bali. The small tropical island in Indonesia sounded lush, beautiful, and fascinating. Captivated, I tucked it away as a wish-list holiday destination.

My family, well certainly Mum, was more deferentially royalist than republican, a bit in awe of the UK as the Mother Country. The Queen was our queen too as part of the evolving Commonwealth of Nations. When I was a child, one of the perks of my mother's job as the only female journalist of the *Chronicle* – 'social editress' – was to attend events welcoming celebrities, usually royal. I remember Mum dressed up in her sparkly pale blue gown with navy straps, to go to the Town Hall for a visit by Princess Alexandra. And when I was about seven, Mum and I stayed at Yarralumla, also known as Government House – home of the Governor-General in Canberra, as guests of Reg, the butler. She must have befriended him after an interview for the *Chronicle*. We stayed in his relatively humble quarters, and I ran about enjoying the huge sprawl of the building and immense gardens and lake.

I went to teachers' college almost by default. English at university seemed daunting; I could have got in with my grades but couldn't imagine prospects beyond university. I couldn't see myself as an investigative journalist, asking searching questions. Slightly panicked, I applied at the last minute to teachers' college, despite having little interest in small children. I survived the two years and then applied for my first teaching post in a distant North Queensland school, in a bid to make my way in the world, away from the family. I shared a flat in Townsville with three young women friends from our Brisbane teachers' college a thousand miles south. We were barely twenty, but we often had to have a lie down after school, so shattered were we by our days with thirty or so seven-year-olds.

For R&R, we did a lot of hanging out at the only wine bar in town. Also, the sandy beaches of Magnetic Island were a twenty-minute ferry ride away for the occasional weekend treat. The subtropical island certainly exerted a strong pull on us; although the name derived from Captain Cook's assertion of a 'magnetic effect' in sailing past it, which interfered with his ship's compass. Most men we met in Townsville were from battalions of army and air force troops stationed there, all in imminent danger of being shunted off to Vietnam.

By our second year of teaching most of the new friends I made were either getting engaged to one of those guys or heading off for adventures overseas. Nothing earth-shattering had happened to me concerning the former, and I was not all that happy with my too-hastily chosen profession. However, I had to continue teaching for two years to avoid paying back my bond to the government for the cost of my training. After that, who knew?

In Maryborough, when I was little, I had perched up on the kitchen sink to jam my ear against the radio for the ABC's anglicized Tales of the Dreamtime, adapted from Aboriginal creation stories. But in our small town then and later in Brisbane, there appeared to be few indigenous people, and those few were usually on the margins. More First Nation people lived in scattered areas further away from the larger towns. Weirdly, like many other white Australians of my generation, I had never met any Aboriginal people. I didn't study history in my state high school but learned in social studies at primary school that a *gunyah* was a shelter built by Aboriginal people, and a *coolamon* was a vessel used by women. I heard black Australian women referred to as 'gins' which is not in any Aboriginal language. It was a pejorative term used by white men. I was only vaguely aware of the early history of Oz and Captain Cook's part in it.

I read later that James Cook, despite his apparent sympathy for the Aboriginal people he encountered, and his instruction from George III to '... take possession *with the consent of the natives* ...', still referred to the country as *terra nullius,* and planted the Union Jack to claim a land that had already been inhabited for millennia. In this 'empty land', about five hundred languages were spoken. The indigenous population retained the oldest continuous culture in the world.

Thus, the scene was set for the injustice, misunderstanding, cruelty, and genocide that followed. The expedient British practice of using the new colony as a dumping ground for convicts from the UK, many of whose crimes were poverty-induced, exacerbated the miserable situation.

Geographically speaking, Australia is the largest of the numerous islands of Oceania, and our closest neighbours are in South-East Asia. We are far, far from Europe on our huge island home. Like most white Aussies then, I was never sure of our national identity and found the world beyond Australia incomprehensible. Yet I was curious enough about our origins to try and check out Europe – reversing the tracks of explorers and colonisers from the seventeenth and eighteenth centuries – with slightly more ease, travelling by plane rather than sailing for weeks over challenging seas. Since the UK had spawned so many of us, and had the common language, it seemed a good starting point for exploration.

When the heady time of liberation from teaching loomed, I arranged to travel to Britain with a friend of a friend via the intriguing Bali. We thought we would try to get a job in catering when we arrived in the UK, then travel around Britain and Europe, probably for a couple of years. Unfortunately, her plans were thwarted by her mother's sudden illness, and I ended up setting off on my own. Of course, I hadn't anticipated the emotional impact of travelling alone, far away from Mum, Dad and Anna. As the plane's engines powered up on the runway, my forehead up against the porthole, I sobbed as my family and hometown rapidly disappeared.

The plane touched down in the capital of Bali, Denpasar. What culture shock: colours, smells, people – and the fact of being an ethnic minority for the first time. Bali was astonishingly different from the Australia I knew, except for its fabulous beaches. The island is a pocket of Hindu culture in an otherwise largely Islamic archipelago. There were volcanoes, rice paddies, and pretty villages of traditional thatched houses; it seemed all Balinese people were beautiful. Elegant dark-haired women with creamy frangipani in their hair balanced offerings of bananas and papaya on their heads, en route to the shrines of Hindu deities. Trailing uphill in their brightly- coloured batik sarongs, they were goddess-like themselves Stepped terraces of flooded rice paddies contoured round hillsides, mirroring blue skies. Near the crater of conical, active volcano, Mount Batur, young hippies were inclined to sit, gazing and smoking weed in a happy, dangerous trance.

There was a painters' village and a silversmiths' village. Another one specialised in wood carving, and I saw old men carving away alongside their grandchildren, passing their superb skills down the generations. Thatched and whitewashed mud huts in the compounds looked just right, as if they had grown there, a phenomenon I attribute to the use of local materials, and simplicity of design. I noticed it later in the UK too, particularly in the Cotswolds. A compound was a community centre for the village, visually simple and pleasing, but carefully constructed to a cultural and spiritual plan.

Each village had its gamelan orchestra. We visitors would hang about outside the compounds and, if lucky, hear a rehearsal of the hypnotic percussive music from gongs, xylophones, and drums – so different with its Eastern inflection. Beautiful young girls danced the *legong* in gold-embroidered costumes and flower-decorated crowns; this dance had been traditionally restricted to pre-pubescent girls in royal palaces. Watching their graceful, complex movements to the quick-slow rhythms of the musicians, you imagined their skeletons had been replaced with wire. Their fingers curved up and back, even their bare toes pointed upwards. Hands twirled, brown eyes darted side to side, as their feet met the floor in complex patterns.

At sunset, we couldn't fail to hear groups of bare-chested men sitting cross-legged around the fire reflected on their faces, performing the *kecak* (aka monkey chant dance). With outstretched arms and flickering hands, they chanted, *ketchuck, ketchuck, ketchuck* – the only musical accompaniment – which persisted throughout a lengthy performance as other elaborately costumed dancers appeared, telling stories from the Ramayana.

Street vendors were everywhere, offering delicious spicy snacks wrapped in palm leaves, with rice that could be white, black, or most exciting, red!

I lodged with families once or twice. My hosts were smiling and kind and made me feel welcome, though I knew only a few words in Balinese, and they had little English. I was delighted to discover a well in the courtyard for bathing, and a recycled plastic bucket for sluicing oneself.

Despite their kindness, the tones and inflections of surround-sound Balinese made me feel lonely after a bit; it was weird to be an ethnic minority. So, although I felt shy, in a new town I would head towards the post office, desperate to find some English speakers. Sometimes I resorted to knocking on doors. I met many nice people on the road less travelled – they all shared a philosophy about keeping eyes, hearts and minds open.

The people of Bali had retained their rich, beautiful Hindu culture, despite being surrounded by a dominant other. I found it particularly striking in contrast with the miserable experience endured by our Indigenous population in Australia. I would happily have stayed longer but my travel plans had me on a plane to Singapore after three weeks.

Singapore was crowded and quite different from Bali, even then a modern, space-age city – colourful, clean, musical and friendly, with tasty cheap food abundant in the jumble of street markets, and many happy-looking lady-boys.

I met a young woman whose boyfriend was in hospital recovering from hepatitis contracted in Nepal, practically a rite of passage at the time. I went with my new friend to visit him. The patient was English, and enthusiastically recommended places to visit in the UK. Adjusting his pillows, he heaved himself up on one elbow to tell me, 'When you're in London, you should head for a restaurant in Hampstead called Bergerac. The food's unusual – macrobiotic – brown rice with everything; very yin yang – Buddhist influenced. It's a great place to meet interesting people. Lots of actors and writers go there. Hampstead's full of 'em.'

2

UK up to 2000 early life and becoming a gambler

Tony

'It was milk, no sugar, wasn't it?' Dave asked, placing the coffee down carefully on the table between us, as the train was moving fast and rocking a bit. 'Yes, thanks,' I replied. Dave is a recovering gambler too, and we met up fairly frequently; not for our regular Gamblers Anonymous (GA) 'therapy' meetings, but for the occasional National Committee symposium. We live in different towns, and today we were off to see representatives of other GA groups in the UK to check that we're all on the same page. No money changes hands, we are all volunteers. I help because I'm so grateful to be out of the total mess my life had become because of my compulsive gambling, and I love sorting things out. Sometimes, however, I had to remind myself that I was not in charge, but just another servant for GA groups.

As he slid into his seat, Dave said, 'I was thinking what a mishmash of life experiences there are in GA. I know a lot about gamblers when they were messed up and then recovering, but not much before. What was it like when you were a kid, Tony?'

It's unusual for gamblers to express curiosity about a person beyond the gambling habit we shared; I wondered briefly if Dave had missed his calling as a shrink. We're a pretty egocentric bunch, even after GA. But I, for one, am thrilled with the refreshing honesty in the groups; I only needed a green light to start talking.

'Well,' I pondered, 'We had some great holidays when I was growing up. Even went skiing in Switzerland.'

'Lucky you! Ours were summers at Margate with a bucket and spade!' Dave said.

'Ha! I like seaside holidays too! But yes, we were lucky. I loved skiing. And we had a big house with a train set in the basement.'

'One of those massive jobs with miles of track and signals?' Dave asked.

'Yep, it was amazing – Dad loved it the most! And with both our parents working, we had a nanny for a while,' I added.

'Blimey! What was she like?'

'Nanny Butler? She was great, I was very fond of her. Kind, but knew how to keep us in line.'

'Family life was so different then,' Dave said. 'I'm guessing you were a kid in World War Two?'

'I must have been about… four, when the war started,' I replied.

Dave told me he was born just after the war, and asked if I could remember much about it. I thought of the time I came across a huge crater in the road where a bus had been blown up and scrabbling about in the rubble with some mates for shrapnel. I thought my dad was a hero as he joined the Auxiliary Fire Service and had to put out fierce blazes during the Blitz. I told Dave how I was packed off to boarding school in Cambridge when I was eight, setting a precedent for my brothers. My parents probably thought a British public school in Cambridge, founded in 1615, with an excellent reputation and a Jewish boarding school, would be a safer bet than bombed-out London.

'I'm Jewish too,' Dave said. 'Jews were scared, weren't they, after the war, even here.'

'Yes, sadly. Did your parents change your name?' I asked. 'Ours had a few incarnations from when my grandfather came from Poland with his family. A registrar somewhere had just written down something vaguely phonetic; then later Dad wanted to sound more English, so he changed it to Howard, like the castle.'

'Right,' said Dave. 'We just dropped a syllable and anglicised the rest. Nobody wanted to sound German or Jewish then.'

I went off for a loo break. Dave had got me thinking about those early years…

My grandfather had started with a workshop at home making waistcoats and became a wool merchant in the East End. Dad joined him, and then my mother and uncle. There had been plenty of entertaining at home when my middle brother and I were trotted out as waiters at bridge parties and masonic gatherings. I'd left school before A-levels. As the eldest son, I was expected to follow in my father's footsteps – the family business. I would have liked to do science subjects, but Dad thought languages would be more useful for communicating with international customers.

I told Dave my recollections when I came back.

'You had to do the Done Thing in those days, didn't you?' Dave said.

'It was normal. I should have stood up for myself more. But I idolised my dad. A bit later I managed to get a diploma in statistics. I always liked figures and systems.'

'Hmm. That certainly shows in what you do for GA,' Dave said. 'Did your dad ever ask you to be a mason?'

'He did, but I didn't fancy it. I think that's when I started disappointing him.'

'Well, they seem a bit weird to us outsiders, I don't blame you.'

He asked about the women in my life and marriages.

'I met my first wife at our local sports club. I was rally-driving with my mate Andy a lot then.'

I told Dave how we enjoyed being on the road together, going to rallies all over the place, alternately driving and navigating We both asked our girlfriends along as cheerleaders for a home rally.

'Did you win?' Dave asked.

'We did! Andy and I were a good team – I still have a load of trophies. Soon after that race Miriam and I were married.'

I thought back to all those years ago when I started working in the family business – my pay was generous, and my salary doubled when they made me company secretary. But in only a few years, the business suffered because of a UK trade deal with New Zealand, making the market for textiles plunge. We didn't have enough in reserve so ended up in the hands of an official receiver. My dad salvaged a few bits and pieces, but I was cast off with no safety net, sinking fast.

'Ah, life, eh! Sounds tricky. So, what next?' Dave asked.

'I got a job with a small business dealing in kitchen chairs; earning a lot less, but I didn't spell that out to Miriam – she was pregnant and wanted our place ready for the baby. I thought I'd be earning more soon – even though my boss wasn't generous. See, I was thinking like a gambler even then, way before I discovered gambling. It was too easy for me not to face the facts.'

'Yep, you sound like an early version of us!' Dave agreed.

'Easy to see in hindsight. We had a nice home, a daughter, and a new baby on the way, but I couldn't afford to pay for everything; debts soon piled up.'

'But you hid your worries from Miriam! That is like me when I was gambling-mad,' Dave said.

'Yes, I wanted everything to be okay, so I pretended it was. Of course, Miriam was always worried about money, but I became good at batting away her questions... Then I had a great new business idea.'

'Ah, what was that?' Dave asked.

'I wanted to make more efficient seating in cafés and hair salons, so I taught myself to do architectural drawings and set up a business, using craftsmen I still knew in the lanes near the old place.'

'Sounds enterprising, how did it go?'

'It was great! I loved it, and it did well, but at the same time, I was struggling with money and ended up borrowing left, right and centre. I just about managed to keep my head above water. Then I had a big success with a café at the Kensington Hilton. The client was so pleased, he invited me out for a meal to celebrate – in a casino.'

I was cut short as the train pulled into our station, Leeds.

Walking back to the station after the meeting that evening, I remembered that visit as if it were yesterday...

I'd never set foot in a casino before. It was the epitome of glamour. Women were dressed up to the nines, their jewellery glittering under the chandeliers – waiters were attentive and the food delicious. It was fabulous. Over dinner my client talked about roulette, an obvious enthusiast, going into detail about how it worked. He asked if I fancied a flutter. I found the numbers and percentages enticing, so I paid for a pile of plastic chips, sat at the green baize table with the croupier, and tentatively placed a few chips on the numbered grid in front of me.

As soon as he set the wheel spinning and the ball started clicking and clacking around, my gut began to churn – excitement needled all the way up to my scalp; I was on high alert. The wheel slowed, the ball clattered and fell... Good God were those my numbers? Yes! The croupier pushed over my winning pile of chips. He sorted out winners and losers and next time I placed my markers with more confidence. The wheel spun and slowed. I held my breath. But again, I won!

Roulette!

I was in love!

Maybe I could sort out my money worries…

I had come home…

I never wanted to leave…

3

London 1968 gambling

Tony

I stepped inside that casino in 1968 and didn't really come out until 1970. Safely in, I could escape from the boring, stressful reality outside. Once at the table, I had eyes only for the twirling roulette wheel. The gambling genie filled my skull. Eventually, nothing mattered but getting back there.

I tried to be sensible. Like a normal person I would set myself a limit, say ten pounds. But unlike that normal person, I would hide extra stashes of cash; in the back pocket of my trousers or inside my jacket, sometimes even in my shoes – just in case… I'd place a bet on my special numbers, hoping for their magic to work, picturing the croupier pushing a winning pile of chips in front of me. My heart would get going in time with the wheel, thumping away in my chest. When the ball slowed and dropped, I forgot to breathe. Had I won?

If the dream came true, my winning chips towered up. But more often they were raked away.

Surely with the next spin, my numbers would come up. No? But they would the next time! Or the next? Such was my gambler's emotional roller-coaster. If I did have a win during the evening, and another and another, I was obviously on a winning streak; with the next spin of the wheel, I'd be able to get that bike for my daughter, pay off the mortgage, buy the family a trip round the world.

However, I regularly worked my way through to the socks until all the money was gone; then sometimes ask for credit from the casino. Anything to stay at the table a bit longer to prolong the slightest chance of winning. Sadly, the losses were far more frequent. The casino *always* wins.

There was one awful night when I'd been gambling nonstop. It was about 2 am. I'd been sitting at the roulette table for hours getting uncomfortably desperate for a pee, but the ball kept settling in my favour, so leaving the table was not an option. I needed to be present with all my willpower to ensure my numbers came up again. There was no way I would leave while winning, which had a predictable consequence. Mortifying! Then I couldn't move until my trousers dried enough to be unnoticeable, which took all night until the casino booted me out. By this time all my winnings had reverted to losses. I had gained nothing and felt horrible.

The outside world ceased to exist in the casino; but as soon as I hit the pavement, I knew there would be trouble. If I hadn't kept enough money for the train, I faced a long walk home; exhausted, sweaty, and filthy. Those treks back were dreadful as reality set in. *How will l scrape together the mortgage that month and find Miri's money for food and new shoes for the children? How? Where was left to get money? Who might lend me some? How could I be so stupid? Again!*

By now the only conversations with Miriam were about money, which frequently turned into rows. I felt like a pressure cooker; home just added steam. How could I keep the wolves from the door while being chased by creditors *and* nagged?! *The unpaid bills weren't all my fault*, I reasoned, *Miri couldn't be organising the housekeeping properly.* Never mind the fact that I was giving her money sporadically. I was making self-justification into an art form. I had a short fuse and escaped by stomping out the door with a slam. The children were quarrelling and crying.

Miriam had no idea at first that I was gambling. Not surprising really, as I was being evasive about everything. Then I started lying. How could I tell her? I was ashamed and could hardly believe it myself. And she'd try and stop me…

I remember another low point in my rubbish behaviour, a year or so after that first casino visit.

'Miri, I forgot. I need to take the car to the garage this morning. I need half of that tenner back.'

Her face fell. 'Really Anthony?! The girls start school again next week. There's so much stuff to get for them!'

'I know. Sorry, but I can't get to work without the car!'

Miriam demurred a bit longer, then marched across the room and snatched up her bag. She frowned into it. 'Where is it? I can't find it! I'm sure I put it straight in here when you gave it to me.' She rummaged around, checking and rechecking. 'I don't understand. It's not here!'

'Don't you sometimes put money in the drawer by the bed?'

'Yes; well, I think I'd remember, but I'll go and look.'

'Not there either!' She reported.

With much less of my usual urgency, I said, 'Let's look everywhere. Sometimes things turn up in the most unlikely places. You've had a lot to deal with lately.'

We searched high and low, down the back of the sofa, in all the bedroom drawers. I even picked stuff out of the rubbish bin in the kitchen. For once I was not impatient but helpful and sympathetic.

Because… all the time I knew it wasn't there. I almost convinced myself it was lost. But I was the culprit. I'd taken it from her purse the day before to gamble with, reasoning that it was only borrowed, I'd replace it straight away with my winnings. But as usual, I lost. This charade was to cover my tracks.

My lying and cheating were reaching epic proportions.

4

London late 1960s my life gets messier

Tony

Even before I discovered gambling, I didn't want to acknowledge money was getting tight, and I was irritable. This conversation is typical of when Miriam was at home with our new baby.

'Anthony, the girls' school outing is on Wednesday, we have to send the money with them tomorrow,' Miriam reminded me.

'How much is it?… *How* much? That's outrageous. Wasn't there one last month? Do they *have* to go?' I said.

'Come on Anthony, do you want them to feel left out?'

'Huh! That school seems to ask for money every five minutes!' I said. 'Oh all right. I'll give it to you tonight.'

As soon as I set foot in the door that evening Miriam asked, 'Have you got the money for the girls?'

'Yes, yes – there you are!' I almost threw it at her. 'Is money all you ever think about?'

Miriam was trying to squeeze money out of a tiny budget, and I was using attack as a diversion. Arguing over every penny became our norm – awful for everyone, especially the children.

After the family business had failed, instead of cutting my losses and adjusting to the new situation, I glazed over the facts and tried to act as if nothing had changed. I still wanted to be the rich boy who could easily provide for his family. My unrealistic attitude to our income made any discussion about money fraught.

Despite everything, Miriam kept our home immaculate, and the girls were always beautifully dressed and charming in matching outfits. When we all went out together, it was usually delightful. On the surface, we had a lovely life. We did manage to live the dream sometimes.

The scene was set, however. I was hoping my luck would change day to day, chasing money, and lying to Miriam while paddling furiously under the surface against an approaching tide of debt and disaster. The night I was introduced to the casino, I was a prime candidate to fall into the arms of Lady Luck.

Once I started gambling, the strain on the marriage was even greater; all I wanted to do was get to the roulette table and away from all the aggro. Normal life was an inconvenient hindrance. I'd stop occasionally, catching a glimpse of the chaos in my wake, and feel stricken and remorseful. Then I tried to be pleasant and conciliatory, but it wouldn't last. I told myself I would not gamble, but neither did that resolve last. There was so much tension eating up my insides. The difficulty of keeping up appearances was taking its toll.

Much later was that night of my big win. The casino was fantastic: glittering lights, cigars and champagne. I'd accumulated a mountain of chips. Magic! I still find it hard to believe I'd summoned up my willpower from somewhere and torn myself away from the table in time to cash them in. £30,000! I was by then very aware of the wheel's power to lure me back; and I managed to dispose of most of the cash, immediately, so it was out of my reach. Methods of disposal that were odd, you might say, when there were so many unpaid bills. I put down deposits on four cars. I've no idea of their makes. Why didn't I buy one car outright? Because that would have been difficult to justify to Miriam, considering all the debts I could have paid off. I just wanted rid of the money – before the impulse to gamble with it became overwhelming. I ended up buying none of the cars, so I suppose that car showroom was just a little richer for my visit. I needed enough money to pay the travel agent for a trip to Japan via America, where my employer had bases. I worked for them selling microwave ovens. I went to my boss presenting the case that it might be a good idea if I represented the company in America and Japan to try and secure more favourable deals with suppliers, I think; I can hardly remember now. Fired up with my win I was an ingenious and energetic persuader, with just a few small distortions of the truth.

I justified the plan to Miriam as a business trip that would be good for my job prospects and probably lead to promotion and a rise. We had not had a holiday in a long time, yet I was to be away for three weeks. I paid a few outstanding household bills. I didn't buy Naomi the bicycle she longed for, with the rationale that every penny counted for the trip. Nevertheless, the remaining money was still burning a hole in my pocket; it found its way out with a few visits to the casino before I got on the plane. Ironically after that huge win, I would have to be frugal on my journey.

Ah, but Las Vegas. A visit there could sort out my cash flow problems…

Despite good and constructive discussions with the company in America and Japan; the casinos did me in. My journey ended up being unmitigated misery compounded by guilt. At the end of my stay in Japan, I'd had to scrape the money together for the train to Haneda airport from central Tokyo as I hardly had a bean left. All the way home I wondered if I'd still have a job to go back to.

When I had the urge to gamble, nothing could stop me. I was a mess of raging, reckless matter, a pressure hose blasting obstacles out of the way. My only purpose was to get to the green baize table and stare at the spinning wheel; to listen to the heart-stopping *click – click – click*, as it slowed; to *will* the ball to drop in the right place.

Later I had been managing a restaurant, Bergerac, and gambling – long before Dianne appeared like a breath of fresh air up the stairs, looking for a job. In no time I was out of control. One weekend when the owner was away, I took some of the restaurant's takings to the casino; thinking I could make up some of the money I regularly lost. I sat there gambling all through the night with the restaurant's money. Madness yes, idiotic and immoral, yes. But in my twisted way of thinking, I had borrowed it. At some point during the evening, I won enough to pay off all the bills and get myself out of trouble. But I was on a winning streak, and you don't jinx that by stopping, do you? I ended up skint, as usual.

When my boss returned on Tuesday he said, 'The safe's empty. You said we had a good weekend, Tony. Where's the money?'

'Oh, I banked it,' I said, heart thumping.

'Well, I have to pay the wages, so let's go and get it!'

We went to the bank together and I strode in firmly.

Believe it or not, I came out with the money, having persuaded the bank manager to give me a loan on the spot. Crisis averted, for the moment. The owner was no fool and kept his eye on me after that. But I didn't get the sack! However, it did stop me from visiting the casino for quite a while.

But I started again, and in no time my gambling was fast and furious, and I was once again in trouble. One night, after plundering my usual hiding places, I borrowed money from a dubious character sitting beside me at the table. And then I kept losing. I lost his money. But I promised he'd have it the following week; despite having no way to replace it. I fobbed him off at the casino once and tried a few more evasive tactics, until he cornered me and said, 'Look mate, I need that dosh, I don't care about your wife and kiddies, that's your lookout. Get me my money or I can't vouch for your safety, or your family's. Do you geddit?'

I got it. If that bloke saw me again without his money, I was in danger of being beaten up, and there was a chance of someone harming Miriam or the children. That kept me away from the casino for months.

But I had messed up our finances so thoroughly that a temporary halt to my gambling wasn't enough to save our marriage. Soon after, messily and sadly, I left the house and Miriam and three unhappy girls, one still a toddler. I went back frequently to put the little one, Ava, to bed. But each time I left she cried so much it was heartbreaking. My finances were wrecked, and I could do little to help my young family with money. No wonder Miriam never forgave me.

5

London 1971 meeting Tony

Dianne

Phoning around from Heathrow on my arrival in the UK, I could only find digs in Earls Court, aka Kangaroo Valley. This wasn't satisfactory, as I didn't come halfway around the world just to meet more Aussies. I was thinking about the snippet of information from that guy in Singapore about the Hampstead restaurant. After three days with the accents of home twanging in my ears, I thought I would seek out Bergerac, thinking I might be able to get a temporary job as a waitress, maybe even find somewhere to live. I tackled the underground northwards and was pleasantly surprised by Hampstead's leafy hills with their elegant, dark brick houses and impressive municipal buildings.

I found Bergerac at the bottom of a hill from the High Street. It was in one of the large, dark buildings but light flooded in from high windows. There was a lively ambience and a plethora of books on shelves. It seemed just as that guy in Singapore had described with its easy and comfortable vibe. Behind the glass of the fresh food counter were colourful combinations of vegetables and brown rice. I liked that, having enjoyed the rice dishes in Bali. Timidly, I asked the smiley person serving if any jobs were going. The girl suggested I ask the manager, who was upstairs, and yes, I could go up and see him, as he had an open-door policy.

I appeared at the top, a blondish young Aussie in my sixties-short, embroidered orange caftan. Tony later confessed to a friend that he'd noticed my legs first, which were probably golden from Southeast Asia's sun. I have my mother's well-turned calves, only thinner. There were two men at desks. I started speaking to the first one, who said, 'Oh, I'm just an actor really darling, I'm *resting*!' He waved his arm towards the other man. 'You need to see Tony here.'

Tony had dark-rimmed glasses and a droopy Mexican moustache. I didn't hold that against him as he looked nice and proved to be friendly and easy to talk to. I may have had a tingle of excitement, even. (He later reported a *frisson*.) I had no experience as a waitress; but since I was a teacher, some nous was assumed. Tony said, 'It won't be full-time, but can you come in for a training session next week? Julia's new here too, but she can show you the ropes by now. If all's well, we can work out some sort of rota.' Great, he was willing to give me a chance. I smiled my way downstairs. The main job requirement seemed to be friendliness.

The staff and customers were interesting and smart. Julia was a music graduate from Trinity College, Dublin, with porcelain skin and sparkling brown eyes, who quickly became a friend and shared my flat for a short time as I'd found an attic bedsit nearby. Tony always seemed to be surrounded by a group of women. I suppose because most of the staff were female, but he was definitely a 'woman's man'. I was flattered and pleased when he asked me out, a couple of weeks later.

6

London 1970s first date, first holiday together

Dianne

My first date with Tony began a bit awkwardly. My new friend from Café Bergerac, Julia, had just moved in to share my attic bedsit for a few days while she tried to sort out somewhere else to live. I was getting ready for Tony to pick me up when Julia came bounding up the stairs. When I told her I was expecting him, she gasped. 'Oh, no! He'll be on his way up. He just gave me a lift home!' She dived into the galley kitchen, hissing, 'Keep the door closed!' (The kitchen was the only place to go as the flat was tiny.) Before there was time to ask why she was hiding and what on earth was going on, he knocked. I opened the door and there he was, smiling, wearing a grey-brown roll-necked ribbed jumper, and the black horn-rimmed glasses, every inch a man you could trust. I smiled back, tucking confusion to the back of my mind.

We set off to Hyde Park for a walk. Wandering round the Serpentine, talking came easily.

'It's great having all this green space in the middle of London. I love it,' I said.

'Me too.' Tony swept his hand towards the gap in the trees of Rotten Row, and said, 'Can you imagine this whole area was taken up by a huge glass building in the nineteenth century?'

'What – for plants?'

'No, for a Great Exhibition – to show off our technological brilliance. It was called Crystal Palace.'

'Wow, what happened to it?'

'They dismantled it and then put it together again on a hill in South London.'

'Oh yes, I think I've seen Crystal Palace on the tube map. Can you see it there?'

'No, it's gone. It burnt down in the thirties. The park is lovely though and has great views of London, but it's a bit of a trek from here.'

Tony pointed to the Albert Memorial. 'That was built because Queen Victoria was so upset when her husband died and wanted everyone to remember him. The exhibition had been his idea. Apparently, he was inspired by an exhibition in Paris, and wanted to show we could do everything better than the French.'

'*Anything you can do…,*' I warbled. 'So that would be why there's the Victoria and Albert Museum and Exhibition Road?'

'Yes, the museum was built later. '

'Didn't you say you live in Exhibition Road?'

He grinned, 'I do, in one of the big houses up from the V&A; but my flat at the top is tiny.'

'Great location though! When I really fell for London, it was near here,' I said.

'Was it? Why?', he asked, skirting around a swan standing on the tips of its webbed toes, flapping its wings vigorously.

'My bus had to stop at Hyde Park Corner for the … um … is it the Household Cavalry? They were crossing over from Buckingham Palace. I could hardly believe how calm the horses were, trotting across that waiting traffic. They looked beautiful – like black satin

– and the guards were so fab in red with their shiny brass helmets with tassels. I was stunned and found it moving.'

'Yeah, we're pretty good at pomp and ceremony in this country.'

'I just loved the colour and spectacle, the power of the horses – that they could make the traffic stop.'

'Are you a Royalist now?' Tony grinned.

'Not quite!'

'Shall we go for a drive through the city? I can show you some of my favourite places.'

'Yes please!'

'Maybe we'll swoop round the East End, where we used to have a business, then see London Bridge and the Tower? The lights will be coming on soon.'

I nodded happily, 'Sounds brilliant!'

While we drove, he explained his marital situation – separated from his wife a year ago. He talked sadly about his children and asked about my parents and sister.

I loved his enthusiasm for the city and marvelled with him at its architecture. He showed me wonderful sights; right through the City of London and the little lanes he knew so well from the wool business years ago; back to Park Lane, Wellington Arch, and along the Embankment where the lights of Battersea Bridge glimmered on the blackness of the Thames. There wasn't quite so much traffic in those days!

Eventually, I felt comfortable enough with him to tell him about Julia hiding in the kitchen. He laughed, embarrassed, explaining he had been on a date with her a few days ago, and she hadn't mentioned moving in with me.

We went to a bar – where he was slightly surprised at my expensive choice of Brandy Alexander – I'd had lots of training at the wine bar in Townsville. We talked and talked, I felt as if I knew him already, and he seemed to know me. It felt comfortable but exciting. We parted with a kiss. I didn't think he'd be dating Julia again.

A few months later we had our first holiday together in Switzerland: '*Knie zusammen*,' intoned the tutor, as, with thigh muscles locked, I desperately tried to persuade the pointed planks beneath me to form a peak together, without doing the splits. Snowploughs! Heavens above! Everyone else on the nursery slopes had been there for a week already. I was almost in tears on this first day, because of being the new girl, with all the tumbles and awkwardness of trying to arrange my feet with their unnatural extensions. However, these nursery slopes were halfway up the Jungfraujoch; by the third day, I managed to join Tony, despite his alarming competence, to continue skiing downhill together. We swooped down through the pine trees past brilliant snatches of green and blue, swishing around to a halt in a blur of white spray. Me, not quite so gracefully. At the bottom was a bar with the reward of warming *Glühwein*.

Another day we got a little train to the 'Top of Europe'. It was so beautiful, so opposite to the flat landscape I came from in Oz. The drama of pure whiteness, the jagged danger, the glory of being so close to the sky, above the world. The breathlessness of altitude. Australia has mountain ranges in the south that get snowed on, but I hadn't been there. My first exciting experience of snowfall was in London. Tony was an excellent skier – great to watch. I'd done okay though. I could see the seductive attraction of the mountains.

7

London 1972 first home together, first mention of the 'g' word

Dianne

I'd spent so much time at Tony's place that my landlady in Hampstead took the extreme liberty of renting my room to someone else; so I thought I'd go the whole hog and move in with Tony.

Our bijou residence was a tiny bedsit at the top of a shabby-genteel Georgian block opposite the Science Museum on famous Exhibition Road. It was a glorious location, but when he'd said the flat was small, he wasn't kidding; to my Antipodean eyes, it was about the size of a cupboard.

It was slightly enlarged by the dormer window – revealing a delightful view of the cobbled side street below. The pastel-coloured terrace of little houses had been rebuilt from former stables. Washing up at the butler sink, one could see the dome of the Brompton Oratory and canopies of London planes. A bath and toilet were jammed together on the other side of a flimsy wall dividing them from the basic kitchen.

We made it cosy on a shoestring. A curtain of red and black Indian cotton defined the tiny lobby area by the front door. An overstuffed bookshelf above one of the single beds threatened to dislodge *The Midwich Cuckoos* and other science fiction favourites.

On a triangular shelf in the corner was a wicker-covered flagon of Tony's homemade elderberry port, with a frequently opened tap. Next to the kitchen entrance was a floor-to-ceiling black knight on red paper, our best result from brass rubbing in country churches.

The building was a friendly rabbit warren of flats and bedsits, and you didn't feel you had to lock your door. It seemed to draw open-minded types from all over the world – not all of them were hippies, though the smell of weed lingered in the halls now and then, most likely harvested from Fred's pot plants upstairs.

I worked in a local pub nearby, tucked away along the cobbled street below our flat. As barmaid and assistant cook, I was learning to reproduce Amy's delicious pub pies; especially the chicken one, with peppers, celery, and onion bubbling under her golden flaky pastry. It was friendly, fun and a bit theatrical – a favourite watering hole of actors, like Jack Hawkins – it was a long time ago. I've always enjoyed London for its celebrity-spotting potential.

One day as morning sun streamed through the kitchen window, Tony sat on a bed reading the paper. I was sprawling on the floor, catching the sun, leafing through another section of the Observer; pleasantly aware of coffee brewing and croissants warming in the oven.

'I love Sunday mornings with you,' he said.

I looked up and smiled into his green eyes, 'Me too.'

A comfortable silence.

'Did I tell you about that time when I won a lot of money?' he asked.

'Don't … think so. How?'

'In a casino.'

'In a casino! Gambling? How much did you win?'

'Thirty thousand pounds.'

'Bloody hell! *That* much! How?'

'Playing roulette.'

'Really? That's possible? Good God! What happened to the money?'

I was sitting up by now.

'I bought a ticket for Japan and put deposits on a couple of cars.' He rummaged in a sheaf of papers. I still have the bank statement. Want to see?'

He'd dug it out earlier when this idea came to mind. It did indeed have the striking figure sitting there indisputably.

'Wow, incredible! Why Japan?'

'I was working for a Japanese company and I kind of engineered a business trip.'

'Have I heard about that? What was your job with them?'

'Selling microwave ovens.'

'Good God Tone, you've done so many different things. Amazing. Do you think you could ever have another win like that?' I grinned, excited. 'Or is it like lightning? Never strikes twice?'

'I believe there are people who have been struck a few times,' he smiled.

'Well, I've still got a bit of savings. What if I give you, say, fifty quid, do you think you could turn that into gold for us?'

Ha, a fateful question, as it turned out. All I knew of gambling was the Melbourne Cup; the day many Aussies would bet on Australia's great horse race, like the Grand National, but without the jumps; and the huge Mater Homes raffles in Queensland. If I lost my fifty pounds I wouldn't be too bothered. In those days one could always earn a living, and an element of risk didn't worry me. I'd come from halfway around the world on my own, after all, knowing no one in the UK.

Tony hid his delight by going to the kitchen to fetch our breakfast. It was the first time he had mentioned the word 'gambling' to me.

8

London 1973 enjoying South Kensington, getting married

Dianne

I loved the way Tony's energy spilled out in all directions. I was delighted with him, where we lived, and London generally. He had so much more experience in the world, with his extra fourteen years. He learned fast and was good at winging it. He would happily talk about anything – whether or not it was his area of expertise. He was fascinated by people and enjoyed finding out how they ticked. When his daughters asked questions, he treated them like grownups and would answer with care, even if sometimes the answers were a bit long for their attention spans. Watching them together was heart-warming. He was kind and would help anyone out. I admired his many practical skills; he was no slacker. Whenever he tackled a subject or a problem, he could see it with a fresh eye, make imaginative leaps, and come up with solutions. He was fun and his enthusiasm would draw you in.

When he was about nineteen Tony had learned to fly in a Tiger Moth. Now he rekindled his passion for flight and planes in our tiny living room in Exhibition Rd, building model aeroplanes with inappropriately large four-foot wingspans; to fly, and demolish fairly frequently, at places like Wormwood Scrubs Park, the 'Scrubs.' Then he would patiently rebuild them. I was a happy witness to this as I shared his pleasure in planes; we'd even been known to drive to the viewing platform at Heathrow to watch them take off and land. This was well before the days of international flights every two minutes.

If the girls had any qualms about their dad and his new girlfriend living in a bedsit, they didn't show them. There were plenty of local places to take them on their fortnightly visits. The lake, birds, and big old trees of Hyde Park were up the road, across from the handsome hatbox of the Albert Hall. Biba, the iconic fashion store of the Swinging Sixties, was a bit further west in a gorgeous art deco building in Kensington High Street. At the other end of Exhibition Road, were the V&A and the brilliant Museums of Science and Natural History. South Kensington station was beyond, with Knightsbridge just a short walk through the back streets, or along the busy Brompton Road.

Tony and Miriam were divorced now, and Miriam had remarried. We did our best to mitigate any discomfort and pain for the girls, and Tony spoke of Miriam only positively in their hearing. I always tried to be normal and friendly to Miriam and her husband. However, she and Tony never managed to get on after their break-up, and both would go out of their way to avoid social interaction. Divorce was much rarer in those days. When the girls were spending time with us, they didn't much like to talk about life with their mother and her husband, and probably vice-versa.

I announced our decision to get married flippantly to my Australian family: 'We're going to get hitched to save on bus fares and please the landlord.' This was fairly accurate, as our conservative landlord preferred opposite-sex cohabitants to be married. In response was a letter from my sister in Australia, which shocked me with questions like: 'How long have you known him? Do you know why he got divorced?'

She doesn't know him. She doesn't trust him! But she's my big sister, and I had given him that money to gamble with… Although that had been six months ago, and I'd almost forgotten about it. Doesn't everyone contemplating marriage have a twinge of doubt, especially if the beloved has been married before?

Tony's apparent failure to produce a glimmer of gold after I gave him the fifty pounds was mildly disappointing. I say 'apparent' because, to this day, I'm not sure if he won or lost. But it was of little consequence to me, except to demonstrate how quickly money disappeared if you gambled it away. It led to one or two conversations about gambling, and how it wasn't such a good idea unless you have money to burn. I assumed I could trust his intelligence and that he wouldn't try it again.

Yet if only I had looked more carefully at the bank statement and asked a few more searching questions about that big win! I had no idea that my innocent flutter could act as a catalyst to set him off gambling again.

My future mother-in-law was never one for subtlety, you could always rely on her for foot-in-mouth statements. When Tony asked how her diary was set on a day in August, and then explained it was because we were planning to get married, she exclaimed, 'Not again!' I was standing there right next to him and felt a bit diminished. It wasn't the greatest encouragement for our life-affirming decision, but we both felt sure of our love for each other and went ahead with our plans.

Tony was a secular Jew, but a strong feeling of belonging was in his bones. His first marriage had been in a synagogue. He enjoyed the traditions he had grown up with, like the Friday night family meal of *Shabbos,* observed in their slightly shambolic, friendly way, at his parents' or brother's house; or *Seder,* the Passover, retelling the story of Exodus. He didn't belong to a *Shul* (synagogue). Fortunately, he didn't feel a strong desire to practise Judaic traditions in our new household. I was agnostic, having lost heart early with the Presbyterian Church and being bored with dragging myself off to Sunday School, though I still thought of Jesus as an impressive role model, tough to emulate.

I'd never pictured myself as a bride. Like many other friends at the time, we were a bit short on cash and didn't see the point of the expensive fuss of conventional weddings. We decided to get married at the Kensington Register Office, afterwards inviting family and a few friends to a small jolly gathering at my Aussie friend's flat in Kensington. I enjoyed being a bride for the day in my cream Ossie Clark pantsuit. We invited the girls and were happy that the eldest decided to come. The younger ones probably felt a bit emotional and awkward about it. My parents flew over from Oz, on their first visit to the UK, which was wonderful.

9

London 1973 cultural coolness, some hints of trouble

Dianne

I was working day shifts in the kitchen and bar at the pub down the road while providing nut loaves for a health food restaurant – we had been married a few months. It was then that Tony first baked bread and made elderberry wine. We were happy, not spending much money, nor saving any. Tony had left Bergerac and was now selling double glazing, which had questionable practices in those days, including cold calling. His sales were commission only, and he was paying maintenance for the children, so there was inevitably financial pressure. He was worried about our future. I thought he worried too much, but then my only experience of being responsible for the lives of children was as a teacher, not a parent.

Tony's brother Graham and his wife, Hannah, were extremely kind, hospitable and welcoming to me as a new addition to the family. We were often invited to family events and gatherings at their place, which were always splendid occasions with Hannah's wonderful food provided with stunning efficiency. Occasionally I would feel a slight chill from one or two of their guests – a disinclination to engage with Tony or me in conversation. Reflecting on this, I imagined that since most of Graham and Hannah's friends and family were involved in the practice and traditions of Judaism,

Tony would have scored negatively for divorcing his Jewish wife, and then marrying 'out'. I was after all a *goy* – a gentile. (I liked the harsher sound of *shiksa*, when I heard it – more New York Yiddish – but its derivation seems to be from the Hebrew word meaning blemish or abomination.) Also, some of the same people might have known something I was yet to find out, that Tony's parents had bailed him out financially more than once, making him the black sheep in their eyes.

I like to think I have a friendly and open attitude to everyone, and this bit of perceived cold-shouldering was uncomfortable and unsettling. It intensified my sympathy for my beloved.

Also, around this time, a little niggle began about parking. Tony drove around Central London and was always keen to park as close to his destination. He usually carried a supply of coins for the parking meters but often dashed away to his errand without inserting any.

'Why don't you put money in the meter? Won't you get a fine?' I'd ask.

'Ah, it's OK,' he would respond, 'I'll only be a minute.'

These minutes incrementally increased, to half an hour, then hours, until he almost always returned to those plastic-covered notices.

One day, looking for a street map, I opened the glove compartment out exploded a great pile of forms. 'Ah, what? Tony! Have you paid any of these?'

Of course not, he just jammed them in the glove compartment and forgot them.

Very early one morning, well before we'd surfaced, there was a knock on the door of our flat. It was a long way up from the front door of the building, so someone must have let the early knocker in. Tony shot up, wide awake.

'Who is it?' he called. No response, but a moment later, more knocking. He called out again. Silence again. Weird.

Eventually, a female voice said, 'Mr Howard I'm a bailiff, can you open the door please?'

He did at last, and she was after money for the unpaid parking fines. When he said he didn't have any in the flat, she offered to take goods in lieu.

'Nothing in here is mine, it all belongs to my wife,' he claimed.

I squirmed, mortified. I can't recall if there was a conversation about proof, but she did tell him that he could expect a summons to appear in court. She suggested that he turned up to avoid imprisonment. This shocked him and left me shaken. So much so that he started feeding the meters and arranged to repay his accumulated fines, avoiding a court appearance.

Life became more uneasy. Small things at first – arrangements were made to meet up with me after work, followed by last-minute phone calls to cancel. It didn't take long for an expectation of disappointment to set in. It was worse when it happened with his girls. Broken dates there meant broken hearts and the danger of broken faith in Daddy. I could imagine Miriam angry on her girls' behalf, but unsurprised.

I thought of the parking fine incidents, and the time I had given him money to gamble with, so I asked, 'Have you been to the casino again Tony?'

'No, of course not, why would you think that?'

'Well, right now I hardly know where I am with you. You keep changing your mind about when you'll be home. And you've called off meeting the girls more than once.'

'I didn't mean to let them down. I'm just so busy at work,' he said.

'Well, they won't understand, they just want to see you.'

I decided to accept his restlessness as work stress. It was a yucky job anyway, although he seemed good at it.

There were his stories too. Tony was a skilled raconteur, and I admired his apparent knowledge of many topics. But there were times, sharing a meal with friends, that I doubted the veracity of what he was saying. It could have been argued that he was reinforcing a tale to make it more interesting. But I was cursed with an inbuilt Aussie bullshit detector and a tendency to call a spade a spade, combined with a suspicion of embellishments. Sometimes I would challenge him publicly about inaccuracies – too abruptly and without grace. I imagine it just made me look immature and shrewish.

Later I noticed his hair looking greasy and stringy, and his personal grooming was poor. If I challenged him about what was so urgent to make him miss yet another meal or outing, his response would be something like, 'Oh these customers are always changing their minds about appointments. But I need their money, what can I do?'

It seemed to me that people wanting double-glazed windows must be an unreliable bunch. It got harder to pin him down to times, even dates. Everything was rushed – he was always flying in or out. He got snappy if I questioned him about it. We'd lost our ease of communication.

At night on my own, I was starting to wonder if he could be gambling, but I still didn't want to believe it. In the light of day, it seemed ridiculous and impossible. But the next time I screwed up the courage to ask, 'Tony, you're not gambling, are you?' He just laughed it off, saying,

'Don't be ridiculous, when would I find time to gamble? Or the money?'

The next time I asked he denied it again, looking hurt. The next, 'I told you I'm not going anywhere near a casino! Why can't you trust me? '

I was getting anxious and didn't know what to believe. But it still seemed so improbable and was so outside my experience that I swallowed my doubts, until the next time.

10

London 1974 doubts and distress

Dianne

Tony continued to work late a lot. He usually told me if he had evening appointments. I was fine on my own earlier in the evening, but after about 11 pm I started to wonder and then worry. *Maybe he'd gone out after work? Why? Where? Surely not to a casino? It wouldn't be another woman – would it?* But I did feel confident and secure in his devotion to me. Because although he got on very well with women and had women friends, he had never shown any sign of being a womaniser.

I didn't like being suspicious; particularly as he could usually deliver a convincing explanation for being late. He couldn't sneak into our tiny place without disturbing me, and his late-night arrivals became more frequent. I managed to swallow some unbelievable stories.

This one convinced me at the time, and only later caused quite a few doubts. I had heard the door when he came in but didn't properly wake up except to ask the time, but in the morning when I demanded to know where he had been he told me this:

'It was crazy. I was tired, trying to leave a customer's house, but this bloke just kept on asking questions. When he gave me the cheque, I almost ran out the door. I started the car, and the fuel light was flashing – stupid – I knew I'd been running on a whisper. I didn't make it to the garage, so I had to walk there with the can.

When I got back there were more parked cars. I poured in the petrol and went to open the door, but the key wouldn't work. I couldn't understand it and tried again. Then I thought to look through a window and saw a notebook I didn't recognize. I finally checked the number plate – it wasn't my car! What an idiot! Green Rover three-litre – identical. Lucky I wasn't arrested!' He did find his car then and had to retrace those weary steps to get more fuel. I snorted a bit with mirth. Looking at him, so exhausted, crestfallen, and wan – I just wanted to hug him. (I mean would you make that up?) I even felt a bit guilty for being suspicious.

However, our home life continued to deteriorate. The slide downhill was bumpy with abrupt stops and starts. Too often he would arrange something and then change his mind. I was less and less certain of his movements. If a domestic problem came up, nothing could be done about it then, as there were always more pressing matters to attend to, like hurrying to work, finding the keys, and needing to be somewhere else. Something Else always had higher priority. The rushing around was distracting and bamboozling. I was doubting much of what he told me, which was unsettling. I hated suspecting that he was lying to me, but it seemed to be what was happening.

Another source of puzzlement was that we seemed to live on bread and cheese. Lovely cheddar and brie mind you, and good baguettes from a South Kensington baker – but a bit too often. Our expenses were not huge even with the maintenance for his girls. On both our incomes our diets should have been a bit more varied. We ate out rarely. It got to the point where if he made any statement, my b-s antennae would shoot up and I doubted all he was telling me. Increasingly I had moments when the suspicion crept in, could he be gambling? I still didn't want to believe it.

One night, when Tony remembered to tell me he'd be late, I was happy enough at first with my own company, intermittently reading and watching television. But it was soon that watershed moment of 11 pm with no sign of him. I'd flicked channels on our nine-inch black and white telly until Carole and her clown faded into pixels. Then I was too restless to relax. I returned again and again to the top of the page of the book I was trying to read, as I hadn't taken in a word. I couldn't make sense of it; my mind was scurrying. *He couldn't be gambling, could he? Not another petrol incident? Why didn't he phone? Could he have had an accident?*

The minutes stretched interminably; it was unbearable. I tried and tried to will him home. It was almost impossible to differentiate traffic on the street from our top-floor flat during the day, but at this time of night, I strained to hear the faintest sound that might be his car. I yearned for his footsteps on the stairs. He's an intelligent man; he wouldn't be gambling! And then, Would he? No, he wouldn't be so stupid! I couldn't quite believe that he'd be at a casino. I was angry at my powerlessness: *How could he waste our money? How dare he! Why? Just like me to marry a loser! I'll end up going home to Oz with my tail between my legs, on my own!*

I hurled my book at the wall, dislodging a couple more Arthur C Clarke's from the bookshelf.

No chance of sleep now. Just agitation. Restlessness. An eternity later I heard the key in the lock. Tony – pale, messy, frowning. I didn't give him a chance to speak.

'Don't tell me! I don't want to hear. You've been gambling. You must be mad! And you've been lying to me.'

As I berated him, I could feel one side of my mouth turning down in bitterness.

'How *could* you, how *can* you do that? With *our* money!'

I was so angry I couldn't get more words out. He didn't try to deny it. He was on the verge of tears himself.

'You're right. I'm sorry. I think I'm out of control.'

'But why? It's so fucking stupid!'

'I don't know. I don't understand. I'm sorry. I don't know what to do.'

11

London 1974 an epiphany

Tony

We were all friends in that building in Prince's Gate. One Saturday I was sharing a spliff at home with our neighbour Byron, both of us mildly stoned. He was draped along the sofa, causing the striped Indian cover to slip down, while I lounged on the cushions opposite.

Byron was appropriately named; he looked just like a poet of the Romantic era and was partly Indigenous American. I remembered Di remarking on Byron's 'Picasso-black' eyes, and his habit of sweeping his dark hair away from them as I watched him do just that. He was a talented songwriter and had written songs for successful mainstream artists in America, while working in Central Park, acting as a mentor for troubled young people.

We both liked talking, not necessarily listening, but this time was exceptional. We were smiling, relaxed with the marijuana, ready to open up with some honest reflective conversation. Byron was talking about his park job.

'Ah Tony,' he said, 'you should've seen the state of some of the guys who turned up at the park, off their heads on drink or crack. So young and in such a mess – you've no idea what we had to clear up in the bathroom. Trying to keep them out of the big house was a nightmare.'

'The big house being … a prison?' I asked.

'Yep, a penitentiary.'

'Are drug problems any harder to deal with than alcohol?'

'Ah nothing in it,' replied Byron, 'both make a shitload of problems and mess to clear up. I was a drinker myself as a matter of fact. But not any more.'

'You were a drunk!?'

'I prefer alcoholic man. It's like – well, it's an illness, an addiction.'

'Sorry, I didn't mean …'

'Ah no man, it's fine, I'm good now, no drink at all. But I was pretty far gone – about to lose everything, could have ended up dead. Being drunk was fine but sobering up was hell. My girl left me, my job was on the line, I was heading for an early grave, just like my grandpa.'

'What did you do? How did you manage to stop?'

'I reached out for help. I went to AA. My girl had tried to get me there before, but I wasn't ready then.'

'What made you ready?'

'Well, I got to the point where I could hardly leave my apartment, went AWOL from work, was barely functioning; stopped looking after myself – I was scared.'

'Christ, Byron, poor you. Was AA any help?'

'It was amazing, as soon as I started talking about myself, they all knew me; it was like looking into a hall of mirrors – 'cause they'd all been in the same place.'

'And that stopped you drinking?'

'It did, because they'd stopped, or were getting there. Those people gave me the guts to try and keep trying. No drinking for me, period!'

'Wow, that sounds incredible, good for you!'

We were quiet for a moment, then I asked, 'Do you think you can be addicted to gambling?'

'Why do you ask that, Tony?'

'Well, I – I gamble. A lot. All the time lately. I can't seem to stop myself. I don't understand it and I don't know what to do about it. I lie to Dianne, and I can't tell you some of the things I've done to get money to gamble with.'

'Hey man that's heavy,' said Byron. 'Yeah, you can be addicted to all kinds of shit, but there is help out there, same as for drinking or drugs.'

'Some kind of support group for gamblers?'

'Yes. Back home there's a place for gamblers who're addicted, like AA – it's called Gamblers Anonymous, (GA). There'll be one here too probably. It'll be in the phone book. It's for real, and it helps. Look it up. I've sent some of our kids from Central Park there.'

'Would it be all young people?'

'Unlikely, most people who end up there have been gambling their butts off for years and years.'

'Are they all down and outs?' The question just popped out of me.

'Thanks, Tony! No. You'll find all kinds of dudes there. And being wasted doesn't make you less human. You'd be amazed at the mix of people digging themselves into a hole gambling. All ages, women too. But most of them get it together at GA.'

'I've got to do something,' I said. 'My life is so messed up; I could end up losing everything again.'

'Yeah, Tony. You've got your Dianne and the girls. Do something about it now, before it gets any worse.'

12

London 1974 finding help

Dianne

After telling me about talking to Byron, and his decision to seek help, Tony managed to stay away from the casino, and he did make a phone call to what turned out to be Gamblers Anonymous, or GA. But no one answered, he said. Maybe the phone wasn't manned, it has a rota of volunteers. It could have been that a volunteer missed the shift for some reason, or maybe Tony hung up too soon. But I was relieved when I got home that evening to hear that he'd tried.

I strongly suggested we phone the number again, together, that night. I got through to a nice man straight away. He introduced himself as a compulsive gambler and asked if I was having trouble with gambling. I explained that it wasn't me and handed the phone over to Tony. He listened intently, then looked up to explain that I could go too and asked if I would go with him the next Thursday evening. 'Of course,' I said, having no idea what to expect, but ready to try anything.

Tony

But I don't know how to live if I'm not gambling. No chance of making the big money I need to plug the holes in my finances. How do I know I won't just miss out on that big win that could solve everything? I can't afford to not gamble… But look at me, I'm a mess. I don't know which way is up half the time. I tell so many lies I don't know what's true anymore. And am I happy? Only when I'm gambling – until I start losing. And that's desperate and miserable again. Half the time I feel crushed, the other half euphoric, elated, like I could conquer the world. It's too much. I can't go on like this. But facing people – how do I tell a roomful of strangers how I've behaved? I've borrowed money left, right, and centre, and stolen it. I'm despicable. I didn't mean to be, but that's what's happened. And what if the girls find out, what will they think? What a mess. Maybe if I can get to the casino just one more time, I'll be able to win the money and make Di happy again. I don't want to lose her. But just one more go, just one more visit to the casino – surely, I can fix this.

Dianne

He doesn't want to go. I know, I can feel it. And I'm not keen on facing a whole roomful of people I don't know – what will they be like? But we must go. We must get to that meeting on Thursday. He needs help – I can't stop him. He keeps saying he'll stop; he won't do it again. But he will, he does. Will this be the pattern for the rest of my life, our lives? If he doesn't stop, I will probably go back home. It won't have lasted long, my married life. But he's still lovely! I'll be all on my own. But I don't want to live like this, it's too miserable. I can't trust him anymore. I don't even like to admit that he lies to me. We must get help, or that's it.

There were still another two days for Tony to get through. If his cold feet told him to find the money to gamble again for one last time, where could he get the money? I was not an option; his parents had had their fingers burnt once too often, and fortunately, he was too embarrassed to ask any of our friends in the building. He already had to find sixty pounds for his employers, as he had gambled with the last customer's deposit money. He was in danger of losing his job. He had nowhere to turn.

On that Thursday evening, I hurried home from work to get ready. As soon as I set foot in the door, Tony said, 'Di I don't think I can do it. How can I talk to a room full of people I don't know about what I've done? It's insane.'

'The way you've been gambling is insane. They must know what it's like. That guy on the phone was really nice and said he'd done almost the same as you. They must be able to help. And I'm coming with you, I'll hold your hand.'

'I need more time to get used to the idea. Maybe the meeting next week?'

'Next week you won't want to go either!'

'I promise I'll be ready then; I'll go.'

'No more promises Tony. We're going now. Tonight. Get your coat. Come on, we're together, I'll be with you!' I said.

Amazingly, we made it out the door.

It was raining, so we walked to South Kensington Station through the museum tunnel.

Of course, there was a delay on the District Line, and, of course, Tony immediately crumpled and said, 'Let's go home, we don't want to get there late.' But I pointed out a viable alternative route on the Piccadilly Line – his bag usually. So, we did make it to the right station and found the address we'd been given.

But where on earth was the actual venue, did we have it wrong? We couldn't find any signs. It's so British – limited signage. Eventually, we found the door to the community centre. Tony looked pale, still ready to flee. I suggested we follow the clinking of spoons and the sound of voices down some stairs. There was a counter with tea and coffee. A tall man with a friendly face immediately turned towards us with a warm, 'Hello! Are you looking for GA? Welcome! I'm George.' He shook our hands firmly in both of his.

'So, who's the compulsive gambler?' George asked after checking our names – first names only. 'Me, I guess,' replied Tony, 'I'm the one who's been gambling my socks off. I don't seem able to stop.'

'You're in the right place mate, I've been there.'

'Been?' I said, 'You mean you've managed to stop?'

'That's right, 'replied George, with his slow grin, 'with a little bit of help from my friends here, to keep me stopped.' He introduced us to a cluster of people with mugs of tea.

We learnt their nicknames: Jim Veg, David Taxi, Dr Ken – very London and charming.

Then we met George's wife Ally, who had the shrewd brown eyes and direct gaze of Julie Walters. 'Hi, cup of tea? We don't go in with the gamblers, we have our own room. They go up the iron staircase there, our room is on the ground floor.'

My feminist hackles rose at this, as there seemed to be only one woman amongst the gamblers. The other women seemed to be gamblers' wives. *Not going in with him? Why ever not? I want to see what happens, be there for him, make sure he stays. I don't really join groups, and this one has a strange name – Gam-Anon.*

Nevertheless, I followed the other women into the room, and there was a scraping of chairs as we settled around the refectory-like table. Regulars were used to sitting in the same place, funny how we're territorial like that. All of them were warm and friendly, and the woman next to me asked if it was my first meeting and we chatted about inconsequential matters and families until we were brought to order by Ally, as she was in the chair that evening. The meeting began with Ally announcing for my benefit, 'Our group is called Gam-Anon, and this meeting is to support you, and all of us in this room. Your gambler is in the right place with the other GA members. They understand each other.'

'When I walked through this door', she continued, 'I'd almost forgotten my name, what with being so busy trying to stop my gambler from gambling.' My ears pricked up as the others murmured in agreement. In Gam-Anon, it seemed, we could learn strategies to deal with the flack that comes from living with a compulsive gambler.

She warned that confidentiality was crucial, to enable people to talk openly about distressing things, often for the first time. Everything we heard at that meeting was to stay within its four walls.

There were readings from the Gam-Anon booklets called *The Twelve Steps* and *Just for Today*. The idea was, that we couldn't stop the gambler from gambling, but we could learn to change our responses. We could become stronger, better, kinder, and more able to see clearly. Much of the advice was akin to what is now commonly known as mindfulness. To help me, as the newcomer, Ally called on a middle-aged woman called Cara, to outline her story. Ally called it Cara's 'therapy', which I learned was the name for one's story in these groups.

All eyes turned towards Cara, who began to speak in her warm Irish brogue.

'Brendan and I have been married for thirty-two years. He was a typesetter in Fleet Street, doing well – he enjoyed working in the newspaper industry. We had a good life. Sometimes we took our three kids to Limerick for the summer. They loved staying with their grandparents – running around feeding the chickens and a couple of pigs, but our youngest avoided the head-butting goat! Brendan liked cooking, and he was King of the Cooker on holiday.

'He always handed me his pay packet – I was best at budgeting, and I put money for the bills in various pots and gave him back what was left. But then he usually handed back a portion for me. That was before I had two part-time jobs. But even after that, he carried on, until … Well, it's hard to pinpoint when things started going wrong. But I do remember the first time he came home with money missing from his pay packet, apologising, saying a mate at work was behind with the rent and was in danger of being kicked out of his flat. 'What about our rent?!' I said. I was not happy. Then it was resolved quickly – Brendan said his friend gave him the money the next day. But it started being a regular thing that money went missing. He got paid late, or he'd manage to lose some – he usually blamed his pockets! It often ended up that I was making up the difference from my small earnings.

'He'd started working overtime, so was coming home later. After a while, even the kids noticed changes in him. He'd been regular as clockwork, but he became unpredictable. My nice, easy-going husband was becoming quite grumpy. He snapped at the boys when he never used to and hated me asking him questions. He wouldn't answer me, he just got more and more evasive. I got to a point when I thought something must be very wrong. I didn't know what to think. Was he unhappy at work? I wondered if he should start putting feelers out to other newspapers, but he said not.

'I didn't know anything about gambling. But to cut a long story short, it got worse, we all got unhappier, and the children got behind in school. I was losing confidence and felt ashamed. I didn't have enough money to pay bills any more and had to creep past the butcher as we owed him a lot and I couldn't pay it. I felt awful and it seemed to go on and on.

'Then one day a couple of years ago, I was in the High Street walking past a betting shop, and I saw him through the open door, putting a bet on the flaming horses!! He must have felt my eyes burning like coals because he looked up and nearly fell off his stool.

He came out sharpish. I couldn't look at him until we got home. And then you can imagine what I said! I was angry and felt like an idiot that I'd never had an inkling; even though I knew of his Uncle Patrick who'd lost everything gambling and died penniless and alone.

'I had no idea what to do about it. But then I saw something in a magazine about problem gambling – there was a group setting up in Central London. I showed Brendan straight away – and suggested we try a meeting. I expected resistance, but he was fed up with himself too – put his hands up and surrendered … He was ready. We got here and we haven't looked back.

Well, it's not all been plain sailing. But he's stopped gambling. Life's returning to normal. The first few months were a bit tricky. He stopped for three weeks then had another bet. It took a few stops and starts, and that made me doubtful again, and we had a few heated exchanges, but now he's got a pin to show he's been gambling-free for a whole year. He was so chuffed! The kids are proud of him, he is gradually paying off the debts, and life is normal again. He's back to being the great daddy and husband he used to be. We come here every Thursday, and he also comes on Tuesday evenings. I had trouble trusting him at first, but I can live without trusting him absolutely because I can trust myself. I can always turn to my friends here for help on bad days. I can love him again.'

Wow! Cara was riveting. I'd never heard anybody talking about a person who behaved so much like Tony, even if there were differences in details. Ally invited others to outline their stories and tell us how they were getting on, and if there had been any progress. Everyone was trying to apply 'the programme,' feeling happy if they had managed a small change. It seemed that before seeking help in this room, a few women had suspected their husbands were having an affair.

Ally began talking about her experience with her husband George. 'My husband couldn't and wouldn't stop gambling, but I'd had enough,' she said. 'So I laid down the law to him. I told him that if he wanted to stay at home with us, he had to go to the meetings, pay the rent, and give me money for the bills as soon as he got his wages. If he missed any, he'd be out on his ear. You can't stop the gambler gambling, but you can lay down some ground rules to stop them from gambling all the money away.'

Not many of us could have done this. I did admire Ally's strength, as an active compulsive gambler wore you down. However, George managed to return to being a nice man even when he was gambling. And he could only gamble with the money left after the mortgage and bills were paid. 'I didn't worry about him anymore,' she said, 'because I knew he was only gambling with money that was left over. Why should I waste my life jumping every time the phone rang or when there was a knock at the door? And in a few months, he stopped gambling altogether. I love our life now, love my kids, have more patience when they're aggravating, and love my friends. I'm getting on better with my job, life's good. I don't want to waste a minute!'

Many people stressed how important it is to protect yourself financially. There were various suggestions of how. We were invited to make use of whichever ideas fitted our circumstances.

I warmed to them all. The atmosphere was so open and friendly. I especially liked the sentiment in the booklet, *Just for Today*, which begins: 'Just for today, I will try to live through this day only, and not tackle my whole life problems at once.'

However, I was anxious about Tony's response to his GA meeting. He's so intelligent, will they understand him? Will he get them? Will he stay till the end of the meeting?

There was time for everyone around the table to say how they'd been getting on. We all smiled wryly in recognition at the tales of pleading, cajoling, ranting, and raving at our gamblers. Some women had threatened to throw their gamblers out, multiple times, but didn't follow through. Once they found this roomful of allies, they realised empty threats were ineffectual and distressing.

It was most common for the gambler to be at rock bottom before he would ask for help. But as Ally had so graphically demonstrated, sometimes before the gambler was ready or willing, a wife or parent may get to the end of their tether and lay down the law. Then the gambler could recognise a new steely resolve in their partner who made it clear that unless he stopped gambling it was all over. He would have to leave the home, leave the family. He understood it as a turning point.

Ally asked if I wanted to say anything. I was aware of many pairs of eyes looking at me expectantly. The atmosphere was charged but sympathetic. I gave them an outline of what had been happening, almost apologising for only having suffered for a year when their distress seemed to have been going on for years. I tried to tell them the things I was too ashamed to tell friends or family and said that Cara's story and what they'd all said rang true in my situation too. I got a bit emotional. One of them patted my hand and offered me a tissue, saying I was in the right place. They pointed out that the length of time didn't matter, but the situation would only worsen without help. The rest of our lives could start now. They were great, suggested I try and come to the meeting the next week, and if I was finding the time in-between hard going, to read one of the booklets I'd been given, or to phone one of them.

A couple of them exchanged phone numbers with me at the end of the meeting, telling me to phone at any time; however, I could hardly get out fast enough as I could hear the gamblers clattering down the iron staircase.

13

London 1974 checking out each other's responses

Dianne

I peered at the group of gamblers spilling out of their meeting at the foot of the stairs and glimpsed Tony talking and laughing! Relieved, I went over to mingle with the small crowd. He introduced me, while I tried to match the gamblers with their partners. They were all smiling.

On the tube on the way home, I stared at him excitedly and said, 'Well, what did you think?'

'It was great,' he grinned, 'I could hardly believe how much they all sounded like me. Well not exactly, but the way they described their gambling – not being able to stop – the things they'd done to get money to gamble with, like seeing myself in a mirror. I could see what would happen to me if I kept at it. A few had even been to prison, and gambling goes on there too – but so do GA meetings.'

'Did anyone else gamble in casinos?' I asked.

'A few, but most bet on horse races or even dogs would you believe! In Walthamstow, they said. But it was the way they kept going back to gamble after promising they would stop, just like me, even after swearing on their children's lives not to. It was a relief to admit to some of the awful things I'd done – and they just listened and nodded.

What about you? How was your meeting?' He asked.

'I felt the same – it was good, they're all so open and honest, and friendly and warm – didn't feel like strangers. But I felt a bit of a fraud for coming after being married just twelve months and most of them have been living with their gamblers for ever!'

'It's amazing any of us still have partners. I feel so lucky to have you. I'm so sorry about putting you through all this my love.' He paused, swallowing the lump in his throat. 'I've been given a second chance, with you, and GA.'

We entwined our hands on the armrest, warm and comfortable, which was nice after the weeks before when I hadn't felt like getting anywhere near him.

'I'm so glad we've found somewhere that can help. A lot of those men have stopped gambling for a while, haven't they?'

'Yes, they're incredible. Dr Ken has a pin for ten years of no gambling! And Jim Veg, five. There was one who hasn't managed to stop but he keeps coming back at least and trying. There's another meeting tomorrow and there are groups all over London. They gave me a list. Will you come again next week?'

'Of course, I'd love to see them all again.'

'Did you find it helpful? I don't want you feeling you have to come with me,' he said. 'But I'm so glad you got me there.'

'Well, you found the number yourself, you just needed encouragement. Yeah, I'll be coming – I want to come back. I didn't much like you going off to another room; but maybe I need help too. I felt a bit nervous telling them about us, but they were all so kind and warm and honest, it was okay.'

I went to bed with my head swirling with the stories I'd heard, ready to believe we could get through this and start to look forward to a happy future together.

Before he came to bed that night, Tony had started a diary.

14

London 1974 GA pamphlet with excerpts from my diary

Tony

Friday 21 June 1974:

I went to Gamblers Anonymous tonight at the Community Centre in Victoria with Di. After losing money two weeks ago I decided to do something about myself and got the phone number from the phone book and admitted to Di that I had never stopped gambling since she gave me that £50 in summer 1972. (And that's not counting the years before that when I *had* admitted I was gambling.) I put off going to GA since then, I blew £15 last Friday, another £40 yesterday afternoon borrowed from Dad under false pretences, and then £60 from a deposit collected from a customer this morning which I had decided to play with yesterday even before I got it. I lost it this afternoon.

Full of trepidation I went with Di to GA. She is fantastic – she says so little but is completely unwavering in knowing what has to be done. When we arrived at GA there were no signs at the entrance, I was ready to go home, but together we went downstairs and discovered that we had indeed arrived at the right place. After a quick cup of tea, we gamblers, about fifteen men and two women, trooped off to a room and arranged the chairs in rows. A chairman sat at a small table in front with information leaflets, and an empty chair for each speaker while they gave their 'therapy'. There was a complete cross section of people of all ages and walks of life.

Dianne was taken under the wing of the women, mostly wives, who went to what they call Gam-Anon, where partners, families, and friends of compulsive gamblers could all go and get help.

I was made to feel at ease quickly, started to breathe more easily, and then the 'therapies' started. One by one most of those in the room came up and sat down facing us. 'My name is … and I am a compulsive gambler,' everyone began and told their sorry stories. It became clear, very quickly, that the big thing for everyone was how many days, weeks, months, or years it had been since their last bet. Then it was my turn. I found it very easy to say honestly what I had done but I knew I was only touching the surface, just talking about the money I'd lost. Despite losing all the time, I was beginning to kid myself that I just needed a bit more willpower – then I could start coming out of the casino winning. Since, I told them, I was almost always ahead at some time. Everyone laughed but they knew I meant it, and without their help, I would go on believing it. Even as I am writing this, I am afraid that when the dust has settled on this series of losses and I get back to having a bit of cash in my pocket, I'll start secretly believing it again. After the meeting, everyone said I should go two or three times a week and I think that's right.

Saturday 22 June:
No gambling – but it's been easy today and no money anyway. I remembered to '…get through each day separately, twelve hours at a time.'

We got up late and Di came with me to Windsor where I had four customers to see. I made two calls but was satisfied to make appointments with them for the following day – quite unnecessary as both would have been prepared to talk to me. What a coward I am. Decided to go to Richmond GA tonight.

Went to Richmond with Dianne. I already don't feel nervous. There is nothing to be anxious about. What upsets me is just going in the door of a public place and asking for GA as if I were branded in some way. The routine here was the same as at Victoria. I feel I am now one of the family. I met one 'five-year man' at Victoria last night who had been three times this week to various meetings.

I had another 'therapy', and admitted I now realised my gambling was incurable and that I am not like those who can go and have a flutter. That pleasure will never be mine. I have learnt I can never take any winnings away so there's no point in trying, and I was a compulsive gambler the day the family business collapsed in 1959 (and not when I first went into a casino in 1969). At that time, I earned only a paltry wage but kept up the same lifestyle of the rich young man from before to please my vanity.'

Dianne: My thoughts on seeing this diary entry much later:
I admired the huge, brave step Tony had taken; in admitting to a roomful of strangers that his gambling behaviour was out of control. It was such a relief to see he had enjoyed the meeting and was happy to keep going.

I can't remember what I did in Windsor when he was busy visiting customers – I hope I was wandering around sight-seeing. And I wonder if I was pleased or mildly perturbed when Tony saw only half the number of his customers. Probably pleased, because then we could have gone to have a nice time at a Windsor tearoom or explored the castle.

We hadn't been out together much for months as he had been working or 'otherwise engaged'. I was happy to accompany him to the Richmond meeting, which was a lot better than if he were to spend the night gambling. There might also have been a whisper in my brain, telling me to escort him to ensure he got there.

Tony: Sunday 23 June

No gambling today, easy … I haven't any money, but when I set out to go to Windsor for my appointments Di gave me a £5 note. I had no worries, but on the way home, feeling thoroughly depressed as I had not made either of those work calls, I did think of trying gambling again. I can't believe I am writing this.

Today has been really bad.

I set out late for an appointment, but I flunked it; bought the paper and sat in the car for an hour instead and then purely for something to do, drove a long way to a park in Watford hoping to meet someone flying model planes. No one there so I went another long way to a park in Luton. Still no one. So I sat in the car feeling sorry for myself for at least two hours, then drove back to Watford. This time there were loads of people flying their planes, but I spoke to no one. I came home and moped all evening.

Dianne

I wonder if he told me all that at the time. Not going to appointments is a step up from not going to work and gambling instead, but if he'd told me I would have found it disappointing. I wonder if he'd lied about it. That is one thing I found difficult for a long time. Truth or lies. Trust or challenge? Partly as our approaches to truth were widely divergent – with my almost punishing Protestant attitude to 'the truth' – examining my every move and motive for honesty and even moral purpose; while Tony was inclined to embroider his stories – perhaps that's a general trait of raconteurs, exacerbated and honed by the secrecy and survival mode of the compulsive gambler. My aforementioned 'bullshit antennae' were far too alert a lot of the time. Had I been a little more mature and surer of myself, I could have tuned out and realised it didn't matter much, it was no skin off my nose. How Tony chose to express himself was really nothing to do with me.

Tony: Monday 24 June:

No gambling and no temptations. Took the car back to the car hire firm. I discussed with them the question of buying a car and filled out an HP form, but I'd have no chance with my record. In any case, I can't afford the deposit.

I don't feel bad. I called the office and told them I'd smashed up the car in the hope I wouldn't lose my job, but I feel free in a way. I don't owe anyone anything now, just thirty pounds-odd to the garage for the tyres and service.

Dianne

This is an odd way of thinking. Was he confiding this to me? It isn't clear from the last diary entry whether he did lose his job, and I'm afraid I can't remember. I found the whole business of selling double-glazing unpleasant as in those days it relied on cold calling and follow-up visits to people's homes with lots of pressure from the salesman, so I would probably not have been unhappy if he quit. His wage was largely based on commission, and a lot of the appointments were necessarily in the evening. Since he was not at all work-shy, and never unemployed for more than five minutes, I would have probably been pleased.

Tony

Reflections after that first meeting:
I'd heard a lot that night about rock bottom. Had I reached my lowest point? Well, the moments of elation after gambling had been brief and always tarnished afterwards, and no, I did not want to be caught up in the endless spiral of misery and stress any longer. I'd heard stories that would make your hair stand on end from some of the blokes who'd been there. It was becoming clear that other compulsive gamblers had behaved madly and badly, even worse than me. But as they delivered their 'therapies', all repeating, with emphasis, (one even bashed the table with his fist) that they couldn't afford to gamble again and that they were only ever one bet away from disaster; I was thinking, in my early, ignorant, faulty and twisted way, *this is brilliant, I can use these guys to get my willpower back. I'll listen and learn, and it'll make me strong enough to go to the casino and just bet with a set amount, and I'll be able to take my winnings away!*

I said something like that, and they laughed. The whole idea was to stop. Cold. Absolutely. From then on. Most of them had stopped – mind you, one did say his last bet had been lunchtime that day! One or two members had a pin in their collars that marked their first year clear of gambling. Dr Ken's pin had a tiny diamond and an X to mark ten years of abstinence. This was incredibly inspiring. He looked happy and relaxed. He was funny, a GP, who had a store of epigrams that it was obvious the others had heard before and enjoyed.

'I'm Lady Luck's Lost Lover – an ex-louse who now likes to think he has a spouse without a grouse', he began. Those around me started joining in as Ken said, 'Every day's a birthday, every day's a holiday, every night's a honeymoon! In the bad old gambling days, if I'd had a badge, it would have had NYSO over BAMN: Not Yet Struck Off, But Any Minute Now.'

After the meeting, I felt an emotional cocktail of happiness, hopefulness and trepidation. My eyes had been opened, I could see that this worked for the people here, most seemed extremely cheerful, even carefree. Unlike me, still in a sweat about how to pay back the money that I'd 'borrowed' from work, which was a customer's deposit. Fortunately, my boss didn't know – if he were to find out I would probably get the sack.

Di and I chatted cheerfully on the train about our impressions of the evening and the people we had met – all positive – so by the time we reached home we both felt optimistic and excited about tackling it all. It was all very well when I was there with all of them – the other gamblers – but the whole idea of stopping gambling, being honest, explaining how much money I owed, later felt overwhelming and I worried (though I tried to hide this from Di) that I would never manage to change my behaviour.

15

London 1974 digesting new sources of help

Dianne

It was post-sixties, and the Age of Aquarius loomed – if only 'peace could guide the planet'. Who could object to the sentiment in that song from *Hair?* Not that I had much time for astrology, though Tony and I both enjoyed the mild diversion of asking questions of the *I Ching.*

It was brilliant that our Exhibition Road neighbour Byron had planted the seed for Tony to seek help to stop gambling. Maybe some will wonder why I needed to go to a group when I am not the one with the gambling problem. After all, I found London pretty friendly and had made some good friends. But revealing this problem to 'normal' friends seemed impossibly difficult, as it was unknown to most people. Also, I was a young Aussie far from home with no relatives in the UK, and Gam-Anon had a friendly, family feeling. The girls lived with their mum and stepfather, so it was easy for us to get to meetings in the evening. I was learning so much from other members of the Gam-Anon group, and I loved the feeling of community.

I had some issues too. My self-esteem wasn't high – it wasn't tip-top before I met Tony. As it sank in that I had married a compulsive gambler, on bad days I'd wonder, why me? What am I lacking? Why do I need strangers to show me what to do? But becoming part of Gam-Anon was crucial to my understanding of the gambling problem and what I could do about it. This message came across in almost every Gam-Anon meeting:

The only human being I have the power to change is myself.

Other pieces of advice that stuck with me were:

Give your gambler space to work things out for himself.
Resist trying to sort him out.
Build on your inner strengths.
Learn to pause and appreciate what you have.
Change what is within your power to change. Let go of the rest.

Tony and I were travelling this route together. It was spiritual in the broadest sense. And our spirits sang in tune most of the time. In both groups, the Serenity Prayer was recited aloud at the end of the meeting. (We both avoided saying the deity word.)

… grant me the serenity to accept the things I cannot change, courage to change the things I can, and wisdom to know the difference.

This made sense to me immediately. It is such a good way to live, for those of us living with a gambler trying to stop gambling, but it could be applied to any life situation. It doesn't take long to work out what can't be changed – working out what can be changed is more challenging. It takes a bit of practice, but it does calm the ruffled spirit when achieved even in a small way.

I wondered how the Serenity Prayer originated and found out that Reinhold Niebuhr, the American theologian who composed this prayer in the 1930s, had originally used these words: 'Father give us the courage to change what must be altered, serenity to accept what cannot be helped, and the insight to know one from the other.'

I prefer 'courage', with the implied action of employing it, and the word 'insight' rather than 'wisdom', as I think it takes forever to be wise. However, what became the Serenity Prayer has more musicality and means much the same. The form we know was adopted by Alcoholics Anonymous, then GA, and many other twelve-step programmes. Precursors of the wisdom in these few lines were the second-century Greek philosopher Epictetus, the eighth-century Indian Buddhist scholar Shantideva, and the eleventh-century Jewish poet and philosopher Solomon ibn Gabirol.

GA and Gam-Anon meetings became our new normal. We loved going. If I couldn't go for some reason, I had what we now call FOMO. Tony grabbed the lifeline of GA and held on tight – becoming one of those in the lifeboat, proffering the line to new members. We both felt that we could share everything with our new friends – even our most embarrassing behaviours, without fear of being judged by the listeners. Being able to be so open and honest came as a huge relief after scuttling around in a state of anxiety. It was hard to reproduce even with close friends. In the raw, early days of recovery, the normal competitive world feels harsh. Not many people understand gambling addiction, especially when there is no apparent physical cause.

Each of the twelve-step fellowships is specifically for one kind of addiction only. Peculiar as it may seem, a gambler cannot go to AA to stop gambling, nor an alcoholic to GA, despite the similarity of approach. They work by identification: *I can see me in you*. Some gamblers with more than one addiction went to two or more fellowships.

The philosophy of GA and Gam-Anon programmes is adapted from AA and Al-Anon. The compulsive gambler should never gamble because he risks losing everything – not just the shirt off his back. The message not to gamble wears off fast between meetings. Like all new members, Tony was offered a mentor he could call.

Most of us find the addictive power of alcohol or drugs easy enough to understand, as the physical effects are visible. That gambling is an addiction is obvious to anyone living with a compulsive gambler, but still tricky to rationalise. A psychiatrist friend of GA explained that when in action compulsive gamblers naturally produce noradrenaline, commonly known as the fight or flight hormone, and that helps to keep them hooked. That visiting psychiatrist came to GA meetings as a friend to observe and to learn.

All of us in GA and Gam-Anon are incredibly grateful to the man responsible for founding the fellowships in the UK, the Reverend Gordon Moody. As Secretary of the Churches' Council on Gambling, he had come across a lot of out-of-control gamblers in total misery but didn't know how to help them and their families. In the early 1960s, he was conducting a service in the Brompton Oratory and had arranged a discussion after the service on 'compulsive' gambling. Fortuitously, an American couple, members of GA and Gam-Anon, were visiting the UK and turned up because the wife had noticed that there was to be a talk on gambling after the service. They were delighted to meet Gordon and realised that together they should be able to set up GA and Gam-Anon in the UK.

The first meeting was in 1964. With his huge energy, compassion, brilliance, charm and wit, Gordon remained a much-loved friend and patron of all of us until his death thirty years later. He went to hundreds of meetings and worked for the rest of his life to spread the word that a lifeline was available for compulsive gamblers and their families in the form of GA and Gam-Anon. He crucially kept the Home Office updated about the catastrophic results of compulsive gambling and set up Gordon Moody House for young gamblers without support.

Today, the ease of online betting from one's phone makes gambling more dangerous than ever. Huge amounts of money can be lost in moments. Feeling despair and shame from huge debts incurred by such out-of-control gambling, some young compulsive gamblers have been driven to suicide. Bereaved parents have courageously instigated the support and campaigning group, Gambling with Lives. The trouble is that tax revenue from the gambling industry is very reliable. Government legislation applied to the gambling industry regarding 'problem gamblers' is minimal and hardly a deterrent.

Open meetings of GA are emotional celebrations for those getting a pin for their first year of abstinence. Helping agencies, journalists, families, and friends can come and listen. Recovering gamblers were always upfront and eloquent about past misdeeds and their continuing recovery, and uniquely expressive e.g. 'the miracle of crawling out of the hole I had dug myself ...' All were overjoyed at their return to normal life after gambling themselves into oblivion. Gam-Anon members were shyer about speaking to large roomfuls of people, being more used to round-table discussions than facing an audience. However, one or two brave souls always got up to talk about life with their gamblers before and after GA. Then there was always loads of food provided by grateful families, helping create a wedding party atmosphere.

I often thought of Ally, the woman who had chaired my first Gam-Anon meeting – about how strong she was, talking about living with her husband despite his inability to stop gambling. 'You will put the money on the table for the rent and the bills, or that's it! That's the end of the line,' she'd said. Her husband George managed to stick to her terms. Despite his active gambling – within a budget constrained by Ally – George was domesticated and kind and still soaked up his GA meetings. When he did manage to stop altogether after about eighteen months, there was much jubilation. He became a most helpful and inspiring example to struggling new gamblers coming through the doors, and that first friendly face we saw, was his.

I don't know if I quite took on board at the first few meetings that the commitment to GA and Gam-Anon would last a lifetime. But GA and Gam-Anon friends are the gold-standard kind you can meet years afterwards, continuing a conversation as if you had left off yesterday.

Tony

As they had predicted, I realised I needed to go to meetings often to silence the demon voice urging me to pay a 'farewell' visit to the casino. Di came to many of them with me – to her equivalent meeting. I was very grateful that she did, and that we were on the same page. We looked forward to going out together each week to meet up with our new friends. I understood from the meeting that it was imperative to face your financial mess honestly and to share the reality of your situation with your nearest and dearest. The literature says that repayments to creditors should be realistic and manageable. One should prioritise keeping the roof over your head, feeding the family, and making allowance for normal expenses, so as not to spread your budget too thinly. But we mustn't leave anyone out, even the smallest creditor. Then we should go and see them all, explaining that we are compulsive gamblers getting help to stop, and offering a repayment plan. Some groups of GA also offered a private discussion on repayment of debt with other couples further ahead in their recovery.

Di had asked me, 'How many people do you owe money to?'

'I think it's just the garage … oh, there could be one or two other small things,' I replied.

Well, that is what I'd thought, and it was very painful as I started to remember one creditor and then another. Dredging up each debt from the sludge of my memory, I fell into a sweat thinking about the lies I'd told as to why I had needed the money. It was hard trying to be brutally honest with myself – and Dianne – and the thought of going to see all these people explaining that I had lied to them was appalling! It beggared belief that I had been such an idiot getting myself into this mess, and how I'd used people. Sorting this out had to be fitted around work as well, I couldn't do it all at once, but the list grew slowly and was comprehensive I thought. By the end of the fortnight, I'd uncovered twenty. (However, further along the path to reality, the total amount had turned into thousands of pounds and would take ten years to pay back!)

It was daunting, but systems were my thing, so there was an element of enjoyment in working out my repayment programme. I laid it out neatly like a spreadsheet, but hand-written within the many concertinaed folds of my Filofax. Dianne looked worried as the list grew but said she was proud of me for doing it.

I went to see the first creditor with my heart in my mouth, half expecting the door to be slammed in my face. To my surprise, this man listened to me, without interruption, and as soon as he grasped what I was trying to say he shook my hand and congratulated me; I could hardly believe that a person could be so nice after I had done the dirty on them. I expected humiliation and instead, it was liberating! What a relief! It was with a humble kind of pride that I ticked my first creditor, indicating their agreement. I enjoyed reporting this at the next meeting.

Eventually, I went to see everyone on that list and without exception they were supportive. By the time I had explained the situation twenty times, I was feeling a lot stronger and much more able to resist that demon voice. And I hadn't gambled. At all. It was miraculous, I felt less anxious, slept better, and even began to feel happy for moments at a time.

Dianne

Some close relatives of compulsive gamblers don't want to go to Gam-Anon meetings. They see themselves purely as injured parties. The gambler was the one who had messed up their lives, it was up to them to go and sort themselves out. It's a shame because Gam-Anon offers understanding, solutions, friendship, and compassion. From the first meeting, I realised how lucky we were to find help early on in our lives together. I'm glad I hadn't got to the point of leaving Tony. Not only because he stopped gambling, but because we both learned so much about life and letting go of things you can't control, from amazing, funny, and kind people. I was encouraged to find myself. If I hadn't heeded this wise advice and had left Tony, feeling angry and let down, I may have gone on to find another partner with problems, as one always looks for a familiar pattern. Anecdotal evidence seems to confirm that there is such a pattern. I would probably have ended up bitter and twisted.

According to other Gam-Anon members, most families' advice when they told them about their partner's gambling was straightforward: Leave him! That is understandable, I was on the verge of that option myself before Tony's miraculous response to GA.

Yet at first, I couldn't help feeling shame – that I had chosen a mate with this big flaw – a gambler who couldn't stop and lied to cover it up. I'd glimpsed an impression of Tony as the black sheep of the family. When I learned that he'd been bailed out by his parents on previous occasions, I understood. This compulsive gambling was an immense problem – of mental health, all bound up with money and trust. But in our Gam-Anon group, it was thought unhelpful to refer to compulsive gambling as an illness in case the gambler adopted an easy get-out such as, 'I can't help it, I'm sick.'

Letting go of the gambling problem and getting back to a normal life required a great deal of trust – which I had to relearn after all Tony's evasive behaviours and fear. One should not be afraid to ask normal questions in a relationship. However, I was learning not to interrogate my partner. As someone in our group pointed out, the worst question you can ask a recovering compulsive gambler is, 'Have you been gambling?' Because if your partner is not gambling and making a huge effort to 'stay stopped', he will be hurt that you have shown you do not trust him. On the other hand, if he is gambling, you are inviting him to lie to you.

Sometimes a member of GA didn't want his partner to go to Gam-Anon meetings. At an open meeting, the wonderful Sarah, Dr Ken's wife, attempted to allay misapprehensions a recovering gambler may have about Gam-Anon:

'We explain to the new member how the force of an addiction surmounts her husband's love for her and their children – and we tell her also from her very first evening, that it will be of no use if she cannot lay aside her bitterness and resentment. How can we begin a new life with these two disadvantages weighing us down? Each of us gives what we can to the meeting. Listening, learning, and passing on our knowledge to others. Gam-Anon is an amalgamation of facts built up over the years of knowledge of compulsive gambling – the problems that follow – ways of dealing with them, and then, finally, the rehabilitation of the person. At no time whatsoever is there any insistence put upon a member to deal with her troubles in any particular way. We only suggest ways that she might deal with her worries which have worked for us. Often various members will suggest different ways they have dealt with the same problem – and it is up to the person themselves to decide what they think may be the best way out of their difficulties. We never, ever, dictate; we only tell of our own experience. And if a member chooses to come to our meetings and take nothing but the friendship they find, that is alright too. At least they have gained that much. They are always accepted, welcomed, and befriended … After years of pulling against one another, isn't it wonderful to be tackling this problem together?'

Sarah was one of the most extraordinary women I have ever met.

Despite any faulty thinking in the first few weeks, Tony managed to stop gambling immediately and kept going to the meetings. We loved the people who enabled this transformation.

16

London 1974 learning strategies from our self-help groups

Dianne

At my first meeting in Gam-Anon, I learned this little mantra that helped me in times of stress. It continues to help me. Like the Serenity Prayer, it's probably incorporated in my DNA by now:

> *Just for today, I will try to live through this day only and not tackle my whole life problem at once. I can do something for twelve hours that would appal me if I felt I had to keep it up for a lifetime.*

I've reduced that twelve hours right down during difficult patches. If I've felt on the verge of being overwhelmed, I can stop, breathe, and think: This will be over in half an hour.

> That little passage is followed by other useful affirmations suggesting that I –
> *read something each day requiring effort, thought, and concentration;*
> *be kind;*
> *have a plan;*
> *find time for myself;*
> *be grateful;*

try to find a moment for stillness or meditation each day;
enjoy what is beautiful.

All much like the wise but often-mocked concept known as mindfulness.

I base my life on the Serenity Prayer. A niece recently sent me a social media post of a Venn diagram reproducing its message: two intersecting circles named 'things that matter', and 'things you can control'. The overlap shows 'things to focus on'.

GA and Gam-Anon groups suggest that the gambler will seek help when he is ready, usually when he's reached rock bottom. Some of us liked to think that our superpower was finding the strength to insist that our gambler should try GA, at least once. If Tony had been any more resistant, I might have been tempted to truss him up like an oven-ready chicken and drag him to a meeting – even though the first step makes it clear that no one, except himself, has the power to stop him gambling.

A partner's or parent's commitment to attend their Gam-Anon meetings could eventually encourage their gambler to try GA, resulting in a happier outcome for everyone. But even if the gambler never goes to GA, the partner or family should at least gain confidence and strength about what to do for their own protection and survival.

Sometimes a gambler refusing to try GA would recognise the difference in a partner's tone of voice when she finally reached the end of her tether. He might go to GA to prevent being kicked out of the family home.

'I still can't trust him,' was regularly heard in our Gam-Anon meetings, from newish members. Well, I trusted that Tony was not gambling, but I had trouble with my accusative antennae again – looking out like a meerkat for anything he might say that may not be quite as I recalled. Sniffing the air for truth, forensically scanning each statement he made for veracity. What a pain I was. He never said anything earth-shatteringly wrong, just chewed the truth a bit, to make it more palatable for me and himself. And sometimes harmlessly elaborated a story just to make it a bit more entertaining for friends. After we found GA and Gam-Anon, the only actual white lie I can recall, was about shopping. Looking at his new shoes, I commented, 'Oh nice, they're smart, I like them! About time you replaced those falling-apart things! How much were they?' The price he told me was very reasonable – he may have said they'd been in a sale. A bit later, troubled by a re-emerging conscience, he volunteered that they were £20 more than he'd said.

'Why did you say they were cheaper?' I queried.

'Thought you might think they were too expensive? Not sure. Didn't think I should spend money on myself when in debt and so on.'

'That's bonkers, you have to have decent shoes – I'd prefer the facts!'

A small thing, which I found irritating because it was alien to my stringently honest attitude. But at least he'd told me, which was progress for him – and I wished I had been grown-up enough to acknowledge that he was trying. A bit later I might have. We all find habits difficult to break.

Because Tony had become used to telling the most convenient lie, he had to re-learn to even recognise the truth. He could hide behind the lying. But he gradually got to understand himself better and became braver and more open. He curbed the urge to make out that he knew more about something than he did. I still tended to look askance at him but tried not to. And he had more understanding about my confidence in him needing to be earned, given his previous damaging behaviour.

I trusted him not to seek out casinos because he was steeping himself in the GA recovery programme – going to two or three meetings a week, using the phone, talking to newcomers and old hands, and taking responsibility for chairing meetings. It was clear that he loved the people and the meetings.

I had, and still have, a tendency to focus on my negative qualities. I was learning to recognise that I had strengths too. When I wanted to do something very much but was hindered by self-doubt, Tony was brilliant at geeing me up.

A staircase of twelve steps is shared by GA and Gam-Anon to help us, still reeling from the recent past, to recover our decency as human beings; to keep reaching for our best lives, hoping we errant human beings can stick to the principles. They certainly helped us to climb out of misery, and to find what gives us joy.

Tony

This is an extract from a pamphlet I wrote for the Step meetings:

Step Two: … *a power greater than ourselves could restore us to a normal way of thinking and living.*

I interpreted this simply for myself: *Stop being afraid and stop feeling alone. Accept that sharing is not a sign of weakness.* But at first, I had to keep coming back to this step to try and understand it. It didn't seem to make sense; my gambling was mine. How could something outside of me stop me from gambling? I only wanted to stop gambling, not be preached to, about the way I lived my life. Finally, the penny dropped. This was neither complicated nor difficult. I just had to hold on to the warmth and friendship that I found when I arrived in GA and remind myself that it was through sharing that I had managed to stay stopped for the first few days and weeks. I just had to stop fighting and start sharing.

> Step Three: *Made a decision to turn our will and our lives over to the care of this Power of our own understanding.* Decisions, decisions. I had spent my life avoiding them, and now I was being asked to hand over my whole life to something, but what was it? I decided to Let Go.

I had absolutely no idea what the power was. I knew that I'd stopped gambling for the first time in my life by sharing and listening in the GA room. The problems I'd caused had not gone away, but there was something outside of me that was helping, one day at a time.

I took a chance and decided to let this something into my life. I was nervous and expected to get hurt and laughed at, but it didn't happen. All I'd done was make a decision. Nothing had changed except my attitude. I was on the way! So, I decided to let go and believe that there is a better way of life possible through the Recovery Programme.

> Step Four: *Made a searching and fearless moral and financial inventory of ourselves,* in other words, looked at myself and my finances realistically. Searching. Fearless. Moral. These words could have frightened me, but strangely they didn't. I'd already admitted I was powerless to stop gambling and admitted reluctantly that my whole life was a mess. I'd stopped running away and had made that simple decision to give GA a chance. It was quite logical that the next step would have me looking at myself a bit closer.

I soon learnt that making a searching inventory could be done one day at a time, in the same way as I was staying away from gambling one day at a time. I broke the inventory down into separate chunks:

character (both defects and good qualities);
priorities and responsibilities;
feelings (good and bad);
finance.

I broke each of these into even smaller chunks. I tackled the easiest first and put off the hardest. Why should I tackle the most painful first? I had a whole lifetime to work on myself.

After looking at the rest of the recovery programme, I also realised that this step was only the process of looking. Doing something about each problem follows later, spread over the next five steps. So painful though some of the discoveries about myself may be, I am being guided to deal with them slowly and surely.

PART TWO

Recovery, life

1975 to 2003

17

Knightsbridge, Madeira, 1974-76 life is good

Dianne

Punctuated with regular weekly visits to GA and Gam-Anon, life settled into our new version of normality. Older friendships carried on too. The year I arrived in the UK, I had a Christmas job stuffing envelopes for the World Wildlife Fund. There I met Maya, who was visiting from Sri Lanka, and Rachel. We all got on and are still friends. Rachel met Richard about the same time I met Tony, and we became a friendly foursome. They eventually went to Scotland to get married, accompanied only by witnesses, making the least fuss about tying the knot of anyone I know. They helped inspire our modest celebration when, a bit later, Tony and I hit the register office.

I felt the wrench when Rachel and Richard moved to Malaysia, where Richard was to teach physics for a few years. But we started exchanging letters and postcards – handwritten, and a great pleasure to receive. They both had a keen eye and a dry wit, so their missives from Kuala Lumpur were often hilarious, even lavatorial – as one day Tony opened a fat envelope from Malaysia to reveal a scroll on soft paper that just kept coming and coming, with regular perforations. Maybe there was a shortage of writing paper in Kuala Lumpur or an excess of bog roll! It was so much fun hearing from them like this, that after they returned to the UK, I was constantly disappointed by the postman. Of course, we had the compensatory delight of seeing them again with their new baby daughter.

London in the seventies was buzzing with creativity. Rachel had introduced me to *The Mersey Sound*, a book by the Liverpool poets, Roger McGough, Adrian Henry and Brian Patten, and to other Northern voices. I loved them for their vitality and wit, still do. Their direct approach to ordinary life makes their work available to all, and great for live performance. Two of their number are still going strong, sadly Adrian died in 2008. Roger is a bit of a national treasure these days, and, as Angela Carter said, 'Adrian's poems sing us away from catastrophe.'

I still had the percussive gamelan music in my head from Bali, and a lot of London-based composers were incorporating it experimentally. Tony and I were fascinated by music from all over the world. At the Commonwealth Institute in Holland Park, we had the privilege of seeing two very different musical traditions come together. Playing sitar and violin, the two superb instrumentalists Ravi Shankar and Yehudi Menuhin interwove Eastern and Western harmonies to create a magical new raga.

Tony inspired me with enthusiasm for jazz of the thirties from his dad's collection of LPs, and I was captivated by ragtime when I was hired as a silver service waitress, at the wake of a transatlantic poet. On hearing Joshua Rifkin belting out Scott Joplin's Maple Leaf Rag on piano, I fell in love with its syncopated honky-tonk rhythm. Considering that we also had a growing interest in classical music, it was a bit of a waste of the Albert Hall's proximity that we didn't take advantage of the BBC Proms. But we spent many hours exploring the great museums of South Kensington with the girls.

Tony's parents could see him becoming a hard-working mensch – which they mainly, I think unfairly, attributed to life with me. It certainly helped that he and I were singing from the same hymn sheet, but his success in turning his life around was down to his own diligent effort and GA. (Although it did seem to be the case that GA members who had the greatest success in keeping their addiction at bay tended to be those with loved ones involved in Gam-Anon.) We were all a whole lot happier than when we first turned up with our hearts in our mouths – miracles can happen!

Tony's mum and dad were impressed enough to invite him to join the new family firm. When I say 'new', it had been established over a decade before by his mother, developed from her hobby of bringing back needlepoint kits from Madeira where they frequently holidayed. A German artist who had settled on the Portuguese island in the nineteen-thirties had helped to commercialise one of the existing cottage industries, needlepoint-tapestry making.

Tony and I went to Madeira for a working holiday. We took a moment to recover from the fright of landing on the little runway hugging the mountains for the length of a cricket pitch and ending on a cliff edge over the sea, before visiting one of the needlepoint workshops, where I was in for a surprise at their extraordinary skills. The workers all seemed happy. A woman looked up smiling to take a design we proffered. Our design was a segment of the Paolo Uccello painting of *St George and the Dragon*, with the princess in peril from the dragon and George in armour with his lance on a rearing white horse. Threading her needle with wool, she began then and there to 'paint' the picture with the needle and thread. No preliminary drawing, just straight in there, recreating the whole image. The woman's hand-eye coordination was astonishing. The feeling of the original was all there. Other workers would copy this model to make a design on canvas mesh with horizontal tacking stitches in coloured wool – to show where to put each stitch, making it easy for the customer to get right, like 3D painting by numbers. They just had to follow the lines with their stitches to produce an impressive, luxurious finish. It felt like all their own work, which it was, in a sense, and it takes ages to do a whole canvas faultlessly.

Back in Knightsbridge, their shop had a few famous customers, including an Australian opera singer and a blues singer from the USA. They both liked doing needlepoint when touring. Sitting in the wings awaiting performance cues, they could have their tapestries on their knees, soothing their nerves while filling the tiny squares a stitch at a time, with big wool-threaded needles. Filling in needlepoint tapestries with colour can be pleasantly addictive. Many customers returned again and again to the shop in Knightsbridge for new projects. It was known for its friendly helpfulness; the staff were keen to please the customers, and proud of their excellent service, delivered with a laugh. Tony's mum and dad were at their best serving customers. They also sold tapestries by post all over the world. The street was a great place to explore and shop for crafts, art, clothes and restaurants, preferably with a full wallet. It became a favourite hangout for Princess Di.

When Tony's parents asked him to help run the business, he accepted their offer of a modest wage, to offset the money they had used to bail him out in the past. In retrospect it would have been better if Tony's parents had been on his list of creditors to be repaid a set amount, like the others, at a regular affordable rate. Then his wages could have increased in line with his responsibilities. He perceived a lack of fairness with his salary, causing him the odd ruffled feather. Apart from that the small family firm worked well as a unit. Tony was equally happy chatting to the customers on the ground floor or dealing with administration in the basement. He was fascinated early on with computers, and he had soon transformed the hefty old bookkeeping ledgers into spreadsheets, to make tracking their increasing customer base easier and slicker. At home, however, we had massive drums of information jostling for space on top of all our wardrobes.

I'd had a few jobs by then – in the Knightsbridge pub; simple accounts in a shoe shop; home cooking nut loaves for a health food restaurant; designing for the tapestry business; but mostly waitressing. I did a trial for waitressing in a city fast food restaurant, and was mortified when I didn't pass go, as you were supposed to remember customers' orders to give to the kitchen, not writing anything down. Anxious not to make mistakes, I tried to scribble reminders which slowed me down – I wasn't invited for a second day! I was really impressed with those who managed to get it together for the impatient lunchtime office workers at that fast and furious pace.

I coped better in more conventional restaurants and liked to help people with their choices. Waiting on people, it's easy to spot good people amongst the selfish and shallow. I will always warm to those who treat those serving them as fellow humans, using eye contact, good manners, and a sense of humour. I may always despise the others!

We had favourite customers. 'A bottle of Bollinger m'dear – doctor's orders!' declared 'Mr Bollinger'. He consistently maintained that his physician had ordered him to consume a magnum of champagne daily for his health. We did worry about the state of his liver! He was always delightful, and I hope he outdid the odds and had a long and happy life.

A bonus of working in London restaurants was getting to know fellow staff members from Southeast Asia or Italy or Iran, I loved the international vibe. But the real reason I kept on waitressing was because I wasn't sure what to do next. Eventually, though, I applied to the Open University to do a degree in English.

Meanwhile, Tony was sawing and drilling in the early hours outside the Knightsbridge shop. He had a motoring project on the go, converting our old VW van to a camper. Somehow, he got away with it in that posh location; presumably there were no residents then. We planned to travel and have adventures – the first to Paris and the Loire Valley. The trip was to prove auspicious.

18

France 1975 a significant holiday

Dianne

It had been a long time since Tony had been to France, and he was planning a getaway for us, heading to Paris and the Loire Valley in the newly refitted van, which was making a satisfactory VW thrumming. Transforming seats to a bed was slick and everything could be tucked away somewhere. We'd had fun accumulating all the domestic paraphernalia and I'd made it cosy and private with curtains and vivid bargello seat covers. I looked askance at the Portaloo, but Tony assured me that all the campsites in France had good shower blocks and toilets. He loved reading maps and had sketched out a route.

He did all the driving because I hadn't yet replaced my lapsed international driving licence with a UK one. Travelling with him was easy; he was a confident and decisive driver, and we would natter about anything or sit in comfortable silence, and he seemed to enjoy an occasional jolt of warmth when my hand came to rest on his thigh. Now and then I'd sing along noisily to our cassettes – mostly tunefully, though Tony turned out to be pretty tone-deaf anyway. We were both suckers for the musicals of Rodgers and Hammerstein and Lerner and Loewe. I was almost word-perfect belting out *Oklahoma*, or 'Some Enchanted Evening' from *South Pacific*, but Tony had to help me with the lyrics from *Guys and Dolls* … 'The people all say siddown, siddown you're rockin' the boat …'

He had a penchant for jazz of the thirties and forties and made me chuckle when pitching his less-than-tuneful voice high to imitate Rose Murphy, chirruping, 'I put a nickel in the telephone and called my baby's number, and got a biz, biz, biz, biz, busy line …'

We drove from Calais to Abbeville where, still in the musical groove, we stopped at a bar to sit with the locals and enjoy a Breton singer growling a throaty ballad or two. The bartender filled our tumblers of vin rouge so generously, that we had to take our time gingerly conveying them to our lips.

Then we set off to explore the magnificent cathedral of Rouen, for despite our secular outlooks, we both loved the serenity of old churches and cathedrals – their thick stone walls imbued with the spirits of people seeking solace over centuries. We found the architecture stunning and admired the exquisite artwork of unknown skilled makers. We also enjoyed brass rubbing in country churches. Laying paper over an ancient brass monument, feeling with your fingers to find the incised lines, then rubbing over them with a heelball of wax to reproduce the image made you feel close to the artist who'd worked there so long ago.

Tony thought his language was rusty, but in the car park of the cathedral, a French motorist falsely accused him of damaging his car with our camper van, and Tony recovered his fluency. He talked fast, twirling his hands around in the air. I tried not to grin, impressed by his Gallic-looking remonstrance!

Following the roads near the Seine, we made our way to Paris. Despite all the iconic images of the Eiffel Tower, nothing quite prepares you for the impact of its size when you get up close to the massive wrought iron feet. You have to really crane your neck to see the very top. We climbed the stairs to the second level – to see all of *magnifique* Paris laid out below. A slight drizzle didn't dampen our enthusiasm for the beauty and order of it all. Then we set off for the Louvre and ended up in the west corner of the Tuileries Garden in the Musée de l'Orangerie, where the Impressionists were. It wasn't that busy in the Orangerie and we saw many paintings I had only seen before in art books. At one I stopped dead and stared. It was a Renoir, *Mme Charpentier and her Children,* circa 1878. Tony possibly thought I was admiring the brush strokes. But after some silent contemplation, I turned to him and joyfully announced, 'Guess what Tone – I've changed my mind. I do want to have children after all!'

This came as a surprise to poor Tony after our soul-searching discussions about whether to try for a baby. The girls lived with their mother and her new husband; we saw them fortnightly on weekends. Tony thought the way I interacted with them was great. He'd also said he was willing and happy to have another child with me. But it seemed to me that having the three children in our lives was enough, particularly since the planet was already overcrowded. I said that we didn't need more children to feel fulfilled, and we had decided against it. I'd never longed for children of my own and my interest was piqued only when my sister started having babies. My little nieces were lovely and fascinating, but even in Australia I had been living a long distance away from my sister and family and hadn't seen a lot of them. At the back of my mind, there was probably a niggle about the possibility of compulsive gambling being inheritable. Not having children seemed the right decision for us. I genuinely thought that I could happily live without having children of my own. Mind you, in those days my default position on major life choices seemed to be plumping for the negative. For example:

I'm never going to be a teacher,
never getting married,
not marrying a businessman.

And …

I'm never going to have children.

All of which were ultimately overturned!

However, almost from the moment we'd decided against having babies, my eyes were drawn to dear little children everywhere. They were all sweet, pretty, charming and mostly female. I started feeling as if something in me had closed down. It was all quite vague, a feeling of negativity and sadness, as if I may be missing out on something. Maybe some lack of continuity. This feeling had been lurking in the back of my mind for a few weeks before we went to France, but I hadn't mentioned it to Tony. I had talked about it a little in a Gam-Anon meeting though, and my friend Sarah, whom I loved for her intelligence, warmth and acuity, commented, 'But dear, are you sure? You would be a wonderful mother.'

'Oh Sarah, thanks, but I don't know; I can't imagine it.'

'Could you not just squeeze one little one into your lives?'

'Hmm, Tony has three already. I think that's enough. But it's nice of you to think I could be a mum.'

When I came across that little girl in the Renoir painting in Paris, I was struck by how much she resembled my Aunty Marjory when she was about six, in a sepia photograph that had always hung in our home in Oz. A little girl with wavy fair hair, Marjory was in a white smocked dress looking down at the flower in her hand. She was my mother's only sister in their family of six children. But soon after this photograph was taken, she'd been killed in one of the first traffic accidents in Melbourne. The little girl in the painting had the same sweet look as Marjory and was gazing at her older sister. I felt a lurch in my chest. And there was Tony right beside me to share my change of heart. We had a private moment of joy in that very public space.

I have only just been enlightened about the gender of the 'little girl'. I never noticed before that the children in the painting are Georgette-Berthe and Paul-Emile, a boy! Apparently amongst the well-to-do, it was the fashion to dress children alike when they were young.

So it was thanks to Paris, Renoir, Sarah in Gam-Anon, all the sweet little children I had seen, and my adaptable partner, that we did go for a baby. Best decision ever. We bought a print of the painting – an enlarged detail – which remained with us for years.

19

Knightsbridge, Hammersmith 1977, new home and baby

Dianne

To check whether I could practise as a teacher in the UK, I had taken the precaution of writing to the Department of Education and Science before I left Oz, and they'd told me I could. But I didn't look for teaching posts as I didn't want to be responsible for ruining any small children's lives by teaching resentfully. (I couldn't wait to stop, in Australia.) I fancied the idea of further study. In the halcyon days of the seventies, there were loads of inexpensive options available for further education. In Queensland Teachers' Colleges, you get a diploma. I wanted a degree. By then I'd worked a bit too long as a waitress and needed to prove to myself I could manage a degree course. I'd also asked the Open University if some part-time studies I'd done in English and Psychology at James Cook University in North Queensland counted towards an OU degree. On our return from France, I had a reply saying that they would work as a credit.

But after we visited France, it seemed that almost as soon as I came off the pill, I was pregnant. We were very excited. I decided not to complete my application for a degree course just then, as I couldn't see myself studying with a new baby. I don't have the steel of Margaret Thatcher, who managed to finish her postgraduate law degree while pregnant with twins.

At the restaurant, they were sympathetic to my new status as an expectant mum. I wasn't sick and felt great throughout my pregnancy. People opened doors for me and were kind. As my bump began to fill the white shirt of my waitress uniform, everything became a bit more awkward. One day as I opened the swing doors from kitchen to restaurant with my bum and a trayful of drinks, I wobbled dangerously amid nervous giggles. I left soon after, with a few weeks to go to full term.

Tony

Life was busy and happy. Di was glowing throughout her pregnancy, and we saw the girls regularly. They seemed to like the idea of a new addition to the family. I was busy at work trying to modernise the business and increase our customer base, while I was ever more involved in GA and helping with its organisation.

Di had stopped bounding upstairs to our flat, and there was hardly room in our tiny bedsit for baby paraphernalia. We needed to look for a home of our own with more space. I placed the point of a compass on a map of London and drew a circle of five kilometres around the Knightsbridge shop, hoping to find an affordable area within easy commuting distance. Almost everywhere within the circumference was well out of our league; but the western segment contained Hammersmith, which was then downmarket, so possible. We took to house hunting on weekends, and Di explored between work shifts. It didn't take long before she found us a promising little house.

Dianne

What were we looking for? Cheapness. Light. A garden. Shops not far away. A park nearby. Some character and history. And a school.

Imagine my delight at being shown a little terraced house built in 1906 in a small quiet street for our sort of price. The only problem was that it was a bit decrepit and needed some work to make it habitable. There were three primary schools in adjoining streets. I couldn't wait to show Tone.

He loved it too but was worried how to pay for some essential repair work. His younger brother Graham was very successful, and Tony asked if he was willing to lend us the extra we needed. He and his wife Hannah agreed straight away. Fantastic! We were so grateful; without it we couldn't have bought the house.

It was another sign of how Tony's status had improved in his family's eyes.

Wow! Our own home, near a park, not that far from the Thames. I didn't know which was more exciting – acquiring a house or having a baby! It was a three-up three-down artisan's cottage with a low brick wall in front of a bay window that enclosed a space big enough for a few pots, and a garden at the back.

One day, heavily pregnant, I was reading in our camper van outside the house while Tony worked inside. A friendly-looking woman with curly dark hair approached the van with her babe-in-arms. I rolled down the window. 'Hello, I'm Annie and this is William. We live next door – I see that William might have a playmate soon!' She lifted the baby for inspection as she smiled and nodded towards the house to the left of ours. The baby smiled too; he looked about five months old. I introduced myself. 'Would you like to come in and have a cup of tea? she said. 'Wouldn't you be more comfortable?'

How kind. It set the tone for our time in the street, which turned out to be rich in friendly and interesting neighbours.

The front wall would prove excellent for sitting and chatting with those neighbours in fine weather, and soon I joyfully planted a wisteria which still spreads its beautiful lilac racemes all over the front of the house in spring.

Tony

The night Dianne went into labour we were still in the South Kensington flat. The hospital was in Hammersmith, and we ended up speeding there in an ambulance with blue lights flashing, I think because the baby was two weeks overdue. We'd been together to ante-natal classes and had a song meant to distract her during contractions. She'd chosen Ella Fitzgerald's 'Spring Can Really Hang You Up the Most'. I was with her for the birth. She'd opted for no anaesthetic so as to have the least effect on the baby and managed with only a small amount of abuse hurled at me. Singing or chanting did help a bit, but at some stage she wailed, 'I'm not having a baby after all – it's a mistake.' The midwife reassured us with a lot of hand-clutching and brow-wiping.

But the baby got stuck – and an obstetrician turned up with what looked like a giant pair of salad servers. I'm afraid that when I saw him insert the forceps around the baby's head and prepare for action by bracing himself on a chair with his feet up, I almost passed out! (Despite my previous experience of helping deliver my second daughter at home before the midwife arrived.) Awful seeing your partner suffer, as most dads will know, but the baby arrived after a couple more pushes – and it was a boy! He was fine. Though his head looked a little conical for a few moments, he had no injuries, thank goodness. But Di had a tear which had to be stitched. They gave her a local anaesthetic – the only drug throughout the birth. Our baby boy's walking reflex was astonishing to see. The doctor held him vertically under his armpits, and he made walking movements in the cot. He was wonderful, Di was wonderful, it was all quite a relief. Women are so brave. Exhausted, and at last relaxed; we gazed, besotted, at our new addition.

Dianne had assumed she would have a girl, with my history of three girls and her only sister's four daughters. She was quite surprised to find herself with a baby boy.

His first few weeks were in Exhibition Road until the house was ready enough for us to move in. That is after the six days Di spent in the hospital with the baby – it was the norm in those days, but perhaps also a precaution after the forceps delivery.

Dianne

Our perfect little one with so-soft warm skin – I was proud when they did all those tests for newborns – the walking reflex – babies know how to walk! And have to relearn it later, obviously. I loved watching – staring – at his little face and the fleeting expressions – he yawned, I yawned, his features momentarily scrunched – what was wrong? I felt so attuned with him. Ears, eyelashes, fingernails – all examined minutely. His fingernails were long as he had been overdue, and he accidentally scratched his own little cheeks until a nurse suggested mittens.

Those few days in the open maternity ward in the hospital were a really useful learning experience for me who knew nothing about how to care for the little life beside me. The woman in the next bed knew how to change a nappy, the woman next to her had tips on breastfeeding, and a kind midwife was there to discuss my fears about circumcision. Aargh, there was a fraught topic. That Judaic tradition was part of Tony's identity as a Jewish man. And yet I had tried to have a pregnancy and birth that inflicted as little damage on the baby as possible. Now here we were, planning to snip his tenderest part! It was one of our most difficult conversations since finding GA and Gam-Anon.

20

London 1970s a cultural difference, family life, community, school

Tony

My parents, hence, my brothers and I, observed most of the traditions in the Jewish calendar. Friday night family meals for Shabbos, which begins the Sabbath; special Seder meals for Pesach (Passover); and a bar mitzvah, the coming-of-age ceremony for a male child, at age thirteen. I guess all these things gave me a feeling of belonging. I liked the familiar rituals and the music of chanted prayers. I had little conviction of faith but am happy that I grew up with that moderate immersion in Jewish culture. My first wife Miriam was Jewish, so in our marriage we had carried on with the Friday night suppers. However, with Dianne it was enough for me to join the occasional family gatherings and celebrations at my parents' or brothers' homes.

When Di and I got married, some of the extended family turned their noses up at my marrying an outsider, a goy, but the nice ones were welcoming after they met her and realised what a warm and kind human being she was. We had no desire to associate with people who judged everyone according to whether they belonged. My feeling of Jewishness was deeply embedded and emotional, based on our long history, and stoked enough by family gatherings. Dianne was sympathetic and interested in Judaism, but she had explained to me that she was only prepared to do things that made sense to her, and had no wish to adopt any tradition rituals, which I understood, and was more than happy with.

Having a male child for the first time made me wonder whether a man can ever feel Jewish if he isn't circumcised, even though our boy was not properly Jewish because Judaism is traditionally carried through the female line. But we were both open to the possibility that in the future our son might become more interested in the religion. Then he could be accepted by a liberal synagogue. But I thought he would need to be circumcised to feel Jewish. It's an initiation rite, a covenant. It seemed logical to do it when he was a baby and could get over it quickly, rather than waiting until he was a young adult when it might be very painful. I didn't have much of an opinion about the hygiene argument as I didn't know what it was like being uncircumcised.

Dianne

Tony did his best to explain why he thought cutting off the baby's foreskin was a good idea. I was worried and asked a midwife in the maternity hospital what she thought. She said 'Well my dear, there is much talk about it for and against, but I have three sons myself and they were all done as babies, and truly, they hardly noticed! The wound healed up quickly and it's easy for them to keep their penis clean. It isn't performed in this hospital. If you decide to have it done, make sure you find an experienced doctor, it's a tiny op but must have an expert to prevent any harm to your little darlin'.' Her big warm smile made me feel mothered. I did not want to cause unnecessary distress to our little boy. But it seemed important to Tony, in terms of identity. I got that the baby's appendage would look more like his father's, and Tony had never expressed any regret about his missing bit. So eventually I agreed. We happened to know a GP who was also an experienced *mohel*, able to perform the deed safely while saying a traditional prayer to welcome the baby.

Unfortunately, my neighbour Annie was having a garden party when the doctor came to do the *bris* a few days after I brought Paul home from the hospital. I felt like a traitor handing our boy over to Tony for his ordeal in our super-clean bathroom. His grandpa was there too. 'Blessed are you, Lord our God, King of the universe, who has sanctified us with His commandments and commanded us concerning circumcision ...' began the *mohel* (in Hebrew). Tony and his dad murmured the response, '*Baruch atah adonai, elo-heinu melech ha'Olam ...*' I heard this bit often enough over the years to be able to parrot, liking the rhythm of the words. I waited at the back, trying not to weep when little Paul wailed. Surgical scissors flashed in the doctor's hands; it was quick. As soon as it was over I cuddled and nursed our boy, and he seemed OK. Thank goodness I was breastfeeding, so brilliant for comfort. To our great relief, the poor child's wound healed up quickly and easily as I carefully followed the doctor's instructions. We managed that hurdle with no lingering distress.

We settled happily into the house and the neighbourhood. On one side Annie and her family, and on the other, a single woman with a mass of springy dark hair, zero make-up, and the warmest smile – Jane, a physics teacher. The mellifluous sound of her clarinet drifted over the fence regularly, and from time to time the piano and second clarinet of her music group enriched the melody.

Our virgin garden was rose-fragrant with Jane's pink Zéphirine Drouhin which, tangled with honeysuckle and deep blue clematis, wound its thorn-free way through the trellis topping the old stone wall that separated our gardens. On summer evenings we shared the perfume of oranges from the delicate white flowers of her Philadelphus. It was a great inspiration for creating a lovely garden of our own, which we started straight away. A pale pink mass of Clematis montana covered our shed overnight, it seemed.

Tony dug a small sandpit for the boys – because soon enough there was another beautiful baby. Jane was a good friend by then and came to our place to look after little Paul as we sped off in the car to the hospital. This time, after a quicker delivery and no forceps, I spent only six hours in the maternity ward with my newborn. It was great to be back home to introduce the baby to Paul, who, at the great age of three-and-a-half, was very gentle with little brother Richie. The same ritual of circumcision was soon over – fortunately with the same speedy recovery.

The girls seemed delighted with their little brothers. The gender of the new ones probably mitigated any mixed feelings they had. They were still Daddy's favourite girls.

Our central London meetings of Gamblers Anonymous and Gam-Anon were getting a bit crowded, so after Paul was born, Tony and I gathered a few others to set up a local group, in a post-war prefab round the corner from home. Starting new meetings near us was both altruistic and selfish as it meant we added another venue for those with gambling problems while gaining a meeting place on our doorstep.

The building had become a small community centre, an initiative of the local Neighbourhood Council, run by volunteers with one or two paid employees. It provided services like playgroups, classes and meeting rooms. During the week I took Paul there, and later Richie, for a toddlers' playgroup, with a group of friendly parents.

I often had to rock baby Paul to sleep on my shoulder on the evening of our meetings, before a neighbour arrived from our babysitting circle – a network of local parents who paid one another to babysit, in points rather than cash (double points after midnight.) We still went to our original meeting place in central London from time to time, as those lifesaving friends were very important to us. Sometimes they travelled west to us.

Sarah was the friend who'd encouraged me to reconsider having children. Knowing we were strapped for cash, she kindly offered us a baby shower for our firstborn. At that time in the UK, this American concept was practically unknown.

We got to know our neighbours – it was great having Annie and Tom next door with their two boys as playmates for our two, and Jude and Evan down the road with their two daughters. Evan was the first friend I knew whose parents had come over from the Caribbean in the Windrush. We shared our kids' birthday parties in our gardens or at the Neighbourhood Centre.

Mary, a sweet and gentle woman in her nineties, lived alone in a tall house on the corner of our street. Her arthritis and other ailments made walking difficult, so I used to take her to the park with the boys – somehow managing wheelchair and tricycle and toddler. Ravenscourt Park had blazing red azaleas in the summer and behind iron railings, a pond with an island full of birds. Mary and the boys loved throwing food to the ducks, swans and geese and enjoyed the commotion as they all rushed to gobble it.

Of the three primary schools nearby, we chose the one which was the shortest walk away. To this day parents fight to get their children enrolled there. It became popular, largely due to the efforts of the headteacher, a very bright, independent-minded Aussie. He believed absolutely in equal opportunities for all children. On one Open Day, some prospective parents made it clear they were planning to send their child to a public school, perhaps wondering if the primary education they would receive at this school would be adequate for entrance. 'Every child here will get a full, rounded education!' he told them. And later in private, 'I'm not interested in grooming middle-class people's offspring for public school!'

The school was open and accessible to parents, who could even venture into the staff rooms, or walk straight upstairs to see the head. Sadly, now, it's necessarily different. Many of the teachers had special expertise in a subject. In the nursery, it was music. Miss Bartosz sang in such heavily accented English it was a little disappointing when the children didn't take on her Polish accent, though they clearly adored her. Throughout the school, learning was enhanced with creativity – all pupils were encouraged to participate in drama, art and music. The infant teacher taught the children to play an instrument. She gave up many of her lunch hours, choosing to ensure that each child in the school had some expertise on the recorder. Ha, you say, poor parents! But there are worse-sounding instruments at the early stages of learning (the violin comes to mind.) The aim was to engage every child's interest in learning. There were maths and English specialists too.

The headteacher was always doing battle with the education authorities to ensure adequate funding and support for the less privileged pupils and parents. Parents willingly volunteered to help with school events and outings. The children flourished and the school had excellent results. It was the last gasp of ILEA, the Inner London Education Authority. Many parents, like us, made lifelong friends there, and remain grateful to the headteacher for his strong-minded focus on equal opportunities and fun for all the children in his care. He could be rather blunt and didn't suffer fools gladly, and I was slightly scared of him at the time. But we became friends before he retired to France to enjoy his new house, garden and music. I'll always be grateful for the brilliant start the school gave to our children, on his watch.

Tony

No gambling! Life was great and very busy. As the boys started nursery, Dianne opted to stay home with the children and tried to develop a small business. She'd had a working mum, and although neither she nor her sister resented this, they would always have liked more of their mother's time. I was totally engaged with computers and wanted to develop a software company of my own. My parents were retiring and wanted to live away from London. The rates were becoming pretty eye-watering in Knightsbridge, so we took the radical step of moving the business to a little cluster of shops on the main road between Hammersmith and Chiswick. I appointed a managing director for the family business and worked from downstairs to develop my new software company.

I had recruited a young man who had been working for the ANC in South Africa. He liked my concept of finding out what our customers needed from their IT systems and then trying to fulfil their needs as precisely as possible. Other new start-ups were aiming for the greatest profit and were prepared to be ruthless exploiting clients to make their fortunes. Not that we didn't want to be rich too, but we aimed to provide an honest, fair, reliable service, and to streamline each business for its maximum efficiency. We promptly solved any glitches. A win-win situation, we hoped.

Once we'd honed our skills, we loved passing them on to smart young people. Our ethos was inclusive, and Bob and I valued every colleague's opinion. Our staff members were from diverse backgrounds.

We were getting new enquiries all the time. There was a great atmosphere of energy and enterprise – it was buzzing, and very busy. I was always trying to do my bit for GA and handled some calls during business hours. I felt pretty stretched with work, the children, involvement in the community, and the business upstairs needing my help from time to time.

21

London 1970s Jewish humour and food

Dianne

Oy veh! Being a *goy,* I don't have the *chutzpah* to make a great spiel of these *goyesher* reflections. I don't want anyone *kvetching* at me until I feel *meshugenah.* Also, I make mistakes and can be a bit of a *klutz.* I don't want to be a *schlemiel schmuck.* And I don't want for you to *schlep* all the way here and get irritated. So, I'll stop, already!

I love Yiddish-Hebrew words and Jewish humour! The jokes are self-deprecating, yet self-celebratory, often neurotic, better told by a Jew. We had an American LP called *You Don't Have to be Jewish* – humour from the nineteen-sixties, so knowing, witty and droll. One of the sketches within was 'The Reading of the Will', a classic. A Brooklyn accent helps. The deceased has been successful in the usual manner, having made lots of money. The family therefore have the logical expectation of generous endowments to all, combined with praise for the surviving relatives on their achievements. Each announcement gets a murmur of approval, except for the last one, because the recipient gets what he deserves, politely and concisely.

Tony had quite a fund of Jewish jokes. Here's a short one: The audience is settling in the theatre, the orchestra finishes tuning up, and a hush descends. Suddenly a woman stands up and cries out urgently, 'Doctor, doctor! Is there a doctor in the house?' A man a few rows ahead turns round and stands up, 'Yes, madam, I'm a doctor.'

'Ah, doctor,' says the woman, dragging up the young woman in the seat next to her, 'Have I got a daughter for you!'

He had quite a stash of aeroplane jokes as well, with punchlines like 'not another day like yesterday!' where everything that could go wrong with a flight had just done so – disastrously – again. He would get the punchline a little bit wrong sometimes, just enough to ruin it.

'D-a-ad!', the boys groaned, rolling their eyes.

'Daddy-y-y!' the girls moaned, with exasperated grins.

Food was another aspect of Jewish culture I enjoyed with my new family. My sister-in-law, Hannah, is a wonderful and generous cook and hostess. Her 'Jewish penicillin' is to die for – the most chicken-y chicken soup with *kneidlach*, small, light dumplings of matzo meal, egg and parsley. It was super-comfort food and often appeared in times of heartache or stress.

The big square matzo cracker became indispensable in our kitchen, as an excellent vehicle for a dollop of chopped liver (whose slightly granular texture I found more interesting than smooth, French-style chicken liver pâté). Tony and I liked it so much that we made it for our wedding breakfast, the modest little meal we gave our few guests after we were hitched. We probably used *cholla*, a soft sweet plaited white loaf with a shiny top, or bagels, underneath the chicken liver. No doubt there was 'new green', (very lightly pickled cucumber) and gefilte fish balls, with their essential accompaniment, *chrain,* a pungent horseradish and beetroot sauce that wakes up the mild-mannered gefilte fish.

When Tony took me to Reuben's for the first time he recommended a salt beef sandwich. He wasn't wrong – so tasty! I needed all my fingers to hold the generous helping of soft, salty meat in its rye bread, the fattest sandwich I've ever managed. I also quite liked the egalitarian take-it-or-leave-it attitude of the waiter serving us.

The Brits can thank Jewish immigrants for chippies, (fish and chip shops). Battered fish has been eaten in the UK for five hundred years, and it came via European Jews. My parents-in-law took me to the best fish and chip restaurant in London and introduced me to their favourite dish, which was plaice cooked in matzo meal, rather than batter.

Watching my father-in-law's skill in eating a plaice off the bone was a marvel. Plaice is a flatfish that lives on the sandy bottom of the sea. He would consume the top layer of sweet white flesh, neatly turn it over and continue, until only the perfectly intact, clean white skeleton remained. Having witnessed this more than once, I was slightly embarrassed when my parents-in-law took a group of us to that restaurant, including my thirteen-year-old niece, on a visit with my mother from Oz. This clever niece of mine normally had perfect manners; I'm not sure why there was rebellion in the air. She picked up her fish by the tail with her fingers, and as it dangled, bit a chunk out of it, managing to look like a forerunner for the lobster-munching mermaid in the movie *Splash*.

'Put it down, Caiti! Put it on the plate!' protested my poor mother helplessly, as Tony and I chortled behind our napkins. To their credit, my parents-in-law managed slightly lop-sided grins.

Lots of things tasted so good: egg and onion, chopped herring, potato latkes – golden and crispy, not just for festivals; smoked salmon too, accompanied by scrambled eggs in our house. My brother-in-law Graham's favourite was a standard of their mum's, lokshen pudding; Tony loved it too – a bit like rice pudding but with vermicelli instead. Her version wasn't over-sweet – made with marmalade, stewed apple and raisins. If you wanted to show love to any man in that family, you baked him a lokshen pudding!

22

Hammersmith 1980s and 90s our differing attitudes to money

Dianne

I grew up in a household where I felt loved. Both my parents left school early to join the working world, and our mum and dad continued working after having their two daughters; I seemed to have everything I needed. Our holidays were often by the sea at Hervey Bay, and I wasn't aware of any lack in my life. We had a piano that my sister learnt to play, but I was more interested in dance and went to ballet classes. Anna was somewhat older, and much more aware of our parents' world and any straitened times they had with money. She had helped Mother out often with her design and dressmaking skills, earning nothing for herself. She was practical, clever, and determined to have more financial security in her adult life and took steps to make that happen.

My easier experience as a younger sibling led to my more laid-back attitude. Bearing in mind that jobs were easier to come by in the seventies, I felt that you could always get one, however humble, to earn enough money to pay your bills. I had managed perfectly well when I started working and was financially independent. I was never motivated to accumulate wealth and didn't give it much thought.

Before the painful discovery of Tony's gambling problem, I had been puzzled why we didn't have a bit more in our coffers, but post-GA our finances were much improved and more normal, even allowing for Tony's obligation to repay debts long-term. When the children were little, I was based at home, and the burden of bread-winning sat squarely on Tony's broad shoulders. We seemed to manage okay then. He had so much energy, maybe I didn't notice his stress levels.

Tony

Growing up as I did in a middle-class home with everything I could want, including fancy holidays and boarding school, I was a privileged young man. When I joined the family firm, I was well paid – more than the business could afford as it transpired – all our salaries were a bit too generous. When the business failed, rather than acknowledge the reality of the considerable drop in my wages at the new job, I carried on as if there was no change. I wanted to fulfil my young wife's expectations of the good life and keep up appearances too, I must admit. If only I had paid attention to Mr Micawber in Charles Dickens's *David Copperfield* when he sums up his financial predicament:

> 'Annual income twenty pounds, annual expenditure nineteen and six, result happiness. Annual income twenty pounds, annual expenditure twenty pounds nought and six, result misery.'

It didn't help that when I was a young child I'd got away with the odd expedient lie. And I kept practising. So, well before I started gambling, I had taken to hiding exactly what was going on, by omitting things or by being vague. I may not have told many outright lies until I started actual gambling, but after that, it became so messy, shameful and out of hand, I felt there was no alternative, I had to lie.

After joining GA I had to look at myself clearly, unlearn that lying habit and face the money problems head-on. But sharing my innermost weaknesses with another person looked frightening and impossible.

After a long time in the fellowship, I wrote down my experience of attempting the Twelve Step recovery programme in a pamphlet, hoping to help other GA members. This is not directly about money but is about facing reality in general:

'Admit to ourselves and to another human being the exact nature of our wrongs'.

Don't try to avoid this step because you cannot find anyone to share with. If you are having difficulty, ask someone in your group or your sponsor. Or choose a trusted friend, someone you respect, or a professional. Try to avoid asking a member of your family or spouse.

The very first time I chose a friend; I must admit I didn't have the courage to admit everything. But then I had not written down everything either while doing my inventory. However, as I did more of it, I was more willing to share. The release I felt each time I 'got it off my chest' was wonderful. The old saying, 'a problem shared is a problem halved' was certainly true for me.

It was important not to choose anyone who would be hurt by me unloading my guilt. Recovery is a slow process and part of it is the acceptance that it will not happen overnight. I had always wanted the results of everything I did to be instant, and now I was learning that even recovery itself would be slow.

Another step advises me to list everyone I've hurt. I later added, in a note to myself and others, that this should include those hurt by bad behaviour as well as those hurt financially. 'Don't leave anyone out!' I made new lists frequently – even after the first one had been dealt with. New names keep appearing, and old ones are dropped off.

None of this however means that I ever became fantastic at handling money, and my business partner, Bob, wasn't particularly good at that aspect of our business either. Like all the men in my family, I love all the latest technological gadgets and was good at justifying their acquisition to myself, whether or not there was enough money in the coffers. Di and I both liked to splash out on the odd luxury item, such as a beautifully tailored coat or a delicious meal out. I was the musical explorer in the house and found the time to check out and source the best recordings of classical music. I discovered many amazing composers like Arvo Pärt, especially *Spiegel im Spiegel*; Schubert's piano sonatas, and a friend introduced me to Bach's exquisite cello suites 4 to 6. I liked many genres – jazz and soul, sitar from India, and Di introduced me to gamelan from Indonesia. We were in tune and often deeply moved by the same music.

Dianne

There were years of relative financial security after Tony stopped gambling, also some things I did not want to scrutinise. Tony was older, wiser (ostensibly) and more experienced. He had been making amends for his past mistakes for years and I felt comfortable relying on him. It was easy to be a bit complacent. Despite many warnings at my Gam-Anon groups that, even after they'd stopped gambling, many recovering gamblers weren't brilliant at handling money; I didn't have the insight to see that it may have been wise not to trust him absolutely with sorting it out. The trouble was, he was working so hard and trying to do the right things and had so much skill and energy, I trusted him more than I trusted myself, it seems. I might have been a little ostrich-like when money became tight again, because according to the stories I heard frequently at Gam-Anon, most compulsive gamblers who managed to overcome their addictions thrived and generally made lots of money. Tony was on track in many ways, but balancing the books was still a bit precarious.

I had to get older before I understood how much more choice you have with some financial ballast.

23

London 1980s and 90s sculpture, community life, pamphlet for agnostics and atheists

Dianne

On the top floor of another local primary school, Jane ran life sculpture classes in the evenings. Her classes were full in the blink of an eye, so one had to be quick off the mark to enrol. Everyone loved Jane, they still do, and she's still teaching. She'll always be a friend to her students, current and former.

She consistently managed to get good, patient models – willing to sit naked for a couple of hours in unnatural positions most of us would find very uncomfortable. A few were stunningly beautiful dancers, but most had imperfections and saggy bits. I was in awe of the supreme confidence they showed in their own skins, never having felt that way myself.

Jane made minimal interventions as we coaxed some kind of shape from our lumps of clay. Her wooden modelling tool hovered near ours, as she suggested a curve here, a bit less there, enabling us to 'see' better; not dictating, but encouraging us to develop our style. I worked mainly with clay, a few preferred to use wax. After a term, we all felt we'd improved. We felt blessed with her time and attention, and we'd always collect loads of money at the end of the year for her gift, which glowed with our appreciation. I certainly owe Jane for what came next.

I went religiously to her classes for five years and then thought seriously about applying to art college. Jane helped a lot with advice, despite not being utterly in favour of the institutions, although having several degrees herself. A friend who is a superb sculptor in wood helped me develop a portfolio, including a project about women and our often-troubled relationship with food.

I submitted it to the prestigious Central St Martins, then the only London college with a part-time degree course and was delighted to be accepted. It was at a very modest fee in the 1980s; just as well, as I only had a part-time job driving a minibus for an older people's charity, fitted around school hours. Because the course was part-time, it would take five years, which I found a little daunting.

Tony

Our patch of West London had a great community feeling, which we relished and tried to foster. We weren't overtly political but got involved in a few struggles for what we saw as the greater good.

At the western end of Chiswick, three curving railway lines enclose the Gunnersbury Triangle, a wilderness of birch and willow. Over the years it had become home to a huge variety of birds, foxes, hedgehogs and other wildlife. Such untouched green spaces, so rich in biodiversity, are rare in London. In the 1980s the local authority was trying to sell the land for development, threatening to obliterate the little haven. Dianne and I joined scores of local people to argue that this area should stay wild for the species living there and for the education of people, young and old. Chiswick Wildlife Group was created, and together residents of Chiswick, Hammersmith and Acton fought to hold onto the land and eventually won. In 1982, a landmark first ruling decreed that the development could not go ahead because of the land's value for nature. It was a great boost for similar community actions across London. Thanks to a lot more work by volunteers, in 1985 Gunnersbury Triangle became a wildlife sanctuary, where city kids and their families can explore and discover.

We were also involved with the Neighbourhood Council down the road and the governing body of the boys' primary school, not to mention our local GA and Gam-Anon groups, and I was on the GA National Committee. GA doesn't have leaders, but it needs organisational 'servants' and a lot of volunteers to keep the groups linked and coherent. And Gam-Anon is the same. GA has supplementary Step meetings for an individual's improvement as a human being, which I found very helpful, struggling as I was to grow and mature. My big ego tended to get in the way – I did like taking charge!

GA was integral to my survival, and I was intent on working out how to interpret the philosophy for my development into a better human being; so, I gradually wrote down some of my thoughts to help myself, and hopefully others as well.

My pamphlet for struggling atheists and agnostics in GA:

'God of my own understanding'

Is this too threatening? Do you just quietly ignore the use of the word God, and get on with your recovery without it? One of the biggest barriers to my recovery was the God barrier. If I was going to give my life and my recovery over to this power of my own understanding, I had to have a clearer picture of what it was. Here are some of the ways I tried to find out:

First, I tried finding substitutes. Some of them were Goddess, the Gods, Higher Power, the Universe, Mind, Soul, Collective

Consciousness, Magic, GA, HOW, (Honesty, Open-Mindedness, Willingness), Goodness.

Try them, if one doesn't work, try another, or, as I did next, try saying the word God, but just think of one of the substitutes. You never have to say it out loud if you don't want to.

Take another look at each step that refers to God of our own understanding and substitute your chosen word or phrase. Alter the words to make them fit for you and see what the authors of the recovery programme were trying to tell us. I tried all these ideas but, in the end, I just accepted that the word God was just a marker, a flag, a pointer and no more.

Think of the use of the word God simply as an exercise in open-mindedness. Just think, okay, xxx, and keep reading. Allow yourself to experiment with the idea there must be something out there other than you, and it will help to free your thinking.

The GA way is, in essence, a spiritual path, initiated and practised through looking at and sharing an understanding of the recovery programme and its use of the word God. This was nearly impossible for me, conjuring up old, unworkable, unpleasant, or simply unbelievable ideas about God as I was raised to understand Him.

Do not call it God unless that is comfortable for you. Don't pretend to believe when you do not. If you remain forever an atheist or agnostic, so be it, you are no lesser a person than a true religious believer. You will still be able to experience an altered life through working with these principles.

Remind yourself that to succeed in GA, no God concept is necessary. In fact, many of our commonly held God concepts get in the way. Do not allow the rules thrust on us by society to become one more block for you. This is a serious business, and we don't need obstructions along the way.

I have watched members come and go over the years. Members who genuinely wanted to recover were willing to do anything, but who deep down wanted to be fixed or repaired. They could not see that they needed to fix themselves, that GA is a self-repairing programme essentially linked to the need for acceptance of their own inner power.

No matter what your age or your life path, it is not too late or too egotistical, too selfish or too silly to repair yourself and become a better person.
For example, a sixty-year-old, permanently unemployed hostel-dweller is today a valuable volunteer in his local community helping old people and those with learning disabilities. A former accountant struck off and imprisoned slowly recovered his self-respect, then his energy and original status, and finally the trust of his family. A market trader created a new material life, became greedy, lost his way and went to prison, then found God in his church in addition to the GA programme. Members are constantly amazed at the loving, spiritual energy they discover. We just want to be normal, well-rounded individuals. The God of our understanding will help us to find the way, but we still must do the building ourselves.

I am sure deep down our true nature is to be outward in our approach to life not inward to ourselves. We just seem to have so much pressure on us to be strong, self-sufficient, to watch out for ourselves – no one else is going to, that our true nature can't get through. If you are one of those who say, honestly, that you don't gamble but you are still the same bastard (and I hear this many times), then have another go at Just for today. But take it seriously this time. Doing a good turn and not getting found out will make you feel good, and that's just the start of making spiritual contact with your higher power. Take the half an hour to relax, but remember the final words, '… during this half hour, sometime, I will try and get a better perspective of my life…' How long is sometime? A few minutes? A few seconds? It's not much. But don't miss it, Just for Today.

24

Hammersmith, New Forest, Great Barrier Reef, 1980s and 90s

Dianne

L ife was good.

Our Tom was the largest tabby and white tomcat in the world. His disposition, despite his size, was gentle and rather canine. He could curve his feline spine to stretch his paws up to the kitchen worktop and make himself huge to see off local dogs. He was not aloof but loving, with a comforting burr of a purr. We had a routine at night, he and I. There was no cat flap, and I regularly put him outside for the night. He would intuit when it was time for ejection and scoot under the bed. Always in the same place! And every time I would grab him by the scruff of the neck as if he were a kitten and drag him out like a sack of spuds – his submission passive and complete. Then I'd heave him over my shoulder, and he'd snuggle into my neck purring like a lawnmower while I stroked him. Poor boy, perhaps he hoped every night this strategy would avert the inevitable. But how come he was always on the bed early in the morning with a paw tentatively patting my face?

We bought a new van as the children were growing up and found favourite places to camp. Denny Wood was one, with its beautiful trees and wild creatures. New Forest ponies snorted in the bracken, and you could hear beech leaves rustling as we opened the van curtains in the morning. Tony asked the boys what they'd like for breakfast, (knowing the answer.) They chorused, 'Cheesy naans!' Tony wrapped grated cheddar inside little twists of dough and baked them under the grill in the van's kitchen, that toasty-cheesy aroma ensuring none of us could resist. Then we had an idle day exploring amongst the oaks and beeches for stag beetles, all of us fascinated with the variety of mushroom and toadstool forms. The boys climbed trees and jumped over ditches. Resting later with our books, the only sound came from the quietly whispering woods.

On our way home in the van, four-year-old Richie asked, 'Can we have Flowers and Swans?' We were getting better at remembering the words and phrasing of Flanders and Swann's wonderful album of songs *The Bestiary of Flanders and Swann*. As in 'Mopy Dick', 'The bottle-nosed whale is a furlong long, and likewise wise, but headstrong strong, and sings this very lugubrious song, as he sails through the great Antarctic Ocean Blue...'

And 'Mud, mud, glorious mud, nothing quite like it for cooling the blood ...'

The few times Tony and I danced together were at the end of conventions for GA and Gam-Anon, held biennially at various venues all over the UK. They were always uplifting, and the post-supper dancing was cheerful and uninhibited. That was when Tony might demonstrate his idiosyncratic dance move – conjuring John Cleese and Michael Jackson. Standing on one leg, the other knee cocked in front at 90 degrees, he'd shuffle-shunt rigidly across the floor, in astonishingly good time to the music. Every time it cracked me up! He jived well, but with partners other than me, I wasn't good at being led or just wasn't good at jiving; sadly, as I think it's a fabulous dance.

Trips to Oz were rare and exciting. When the boys were about eight and four, we visited my family in Brisbane. We also travelled north to see my uncle and aunt in their Sunshine Coast home.

Auntie Joan tended her sub-tropical garden with love. It was lush with gingers, orchids, and palms. By the patio was a swimming pool.

Tony demonstrated another slapstick turn in the pool – I could call it the Cactus Dive. Standing at the edge on one leg, the other bent up at the back, with a leading arm at right angles, and pistol-like index finger and thumb, he resembled an Egyptian hieroglyph or a cartoon cactus. Then he leaned ever-so-slightly forward and allowed himself, seemingly in slow motion, to fall and crash into the pool. The huge splash and waves made the boys giggle hysterically. I'm still not sure why it was so funny, but I always had to laugh too!

We also had the good fortune to visit Heron Island on the Great Barrier Reef. At that time, the only way to get to the island research station was by a small noisy helicopter from Gladstone, flying with open windows. Experimentally, I stuck out my forearm – it was nearly whipped off in the air stream! From that privileged vantage point, we saw the shadowy shapes of dolphins and turtles in the clear blue-green sea below.

The helicopter landed on the island in a great flurry of flying sand. We trudged up the hot beach, aware of our sandals getting heavier, filling up with fine white sand. A chalet notice advised us to turn off external lights at bedtime. Baby turtles, on their first hazardous journey after hatching and clambering out of their nest holes above the waterline, on their way to the sea, could head the wrong way, towards our lights. The notice also announced that it was good practice to wear a hat to intercept the occasional birdie blessing, as black noddy terns with sleek grey heads loved to roost in the Pisonia trees' low network of branches. You could take avoiding action if you heard their *crick-cricking* in time.

One day we took a boat trip to tiny Wilson Island; like Heron, covered with broad-leafed Pisonia trees, which only grow in coral sand. Their shade was a welcome relief as Wilson Island was possibly the hottest place we've ever been. The seeds of Pisonia are so sticky that small birds can get covered in them – lethal for the bird, but ultimately nutritious for the tree. The boat that motored us to the island stopped short for those who wanted to swim the rest of the way to the reef. Paul bravely chose to swim with me – a long way for a young boy, across seemingly bottomless indigo, to the reef's towering cliff wall. Once over it, we found ourselves in a warm turquoise lagoon. It was a coral garden of glorious colours, and we were amongst a shimmering cloud of tiny silver fish that abruptly changed shape and direction like a murmuration of starlings. A dark manta ray glided ahead on its rippling wings. Little clown fish, vivid in orange and white stripes like Nemo, darted around near large green and pink parrot fish as they chomped away with their beaks on purple staghorn and pale green brain coral. Here and there we saw the blue velvet ruffled edges of open giant clams. We were dazzled by the complex beauty of it all.

It *could* remain the planet's only living organism visible from space; though decades on, the reef is in grave danger from warming seas and bleaching events, acidifying waters, predatory crown-of-thorns starfish, and man-made damage. Excellent people at the island research station, and in various parts of the globe, continue their positive work to prevent the annihilation of reefs.

As I walk downstairs in my Somerset home, there's a large photograph Tony took that day, of the boys laughing joyfully, standing on a picnic table under a Pisonia tree. It still makes me smile. Or weep.

Tony

Something woke me in the middle of the night – it could have been a falling coconut. I checked the tide times with my torch, thinking I'd go to the beach to see if I could spot mother turtles laying their eggs.

It seemed about the right time. Since Di and the boys were out for the count, I crept around them quietly, trying to remember what the guidebook had said: No lights, keep ten metres from the turtles and go behind them when passing. It was still the season, but I was only half expecting to see any. As I reached the beach, I saw the silhouettes of a few people moving about, and when my eyes adjusted to the moonlight, massive forms came into focus making their way up to the dunes at the top of the beach. The flash and plop of sand spray indicated some mother turtles were already digging. They were using their flippers like shovels – making the holes deep. I chose 'my' turtle and found a place to sit unobtrusively. She positioned herself over the hole and I caught a glimpse of white as she plopped out an egg. I stayed a long time, about an hour, and all the time she was dropping her round white eggs into the nest-hole. Turtles lay up to a hundred, I learned. I remembered to look up at the stars from time to time, having a stretch to ease my limbs – thinking of Di a few nights ago. She'd tried (and failed) to drag me outside to look at the Milky Way, to see if it still looked the same as when she was a child. She was right, it was incredible. Seeing the dense luminosity of so many stars made you feel at one with the universe.

Eventually, my turtle laboriously covered up her eggs with sand and I watched her lumber slowly back to the sea, exhausted. I regretted not waking the family to see such a once-in-a-lifetime event – so magical to witness.

However, on a nearby beach a couple of days later, just before sunset this time, we all watched dozens of hatchling turtles scamper down to the sea. Fortunately, they were able to move much faster than their ponderous mothers. The boys were enchanted. We had to cover our eyes from time to time, rooting for the little turtles to make it to the sea on their tiny flippers, as the gulls above cawed, swooping dangerously.

Dianne

At the boys' primary school, the children thrived with creative input in storytelling, music, art and drama. Certainly, our boys did: it was great seeing them develop into rounded human beings. At the end-of-year dramas, we parents had that empathetic churning of the gut, willing our child to remember his lines. Then we'd all be groping for tissues as soon as the actors appeared on stage to deliver their line or two. One of the teachers had been an actor himself and was a director par excellence. One year he produced a little-known musical called *The Matchgirls*, based on the true story of a historic strike by women in a match factory, because of conditions dangerous to the workers. Our boy Paul played an obstructive foreman with a notepad, dressed in a bowler hat and braces. For a baddie, he looked rather sweet! Oddly enough, years later, Tony's brother Graham instigated a development project that turned the former Bryant and May match factory into homes.

The only other time we saw Paul acting in public was in his A-level year, as Biff Loman, the older son of the tragic character Willy, in *Death of a Salesman*. It was mesmerising. I stopped seeing my son on the stage and could only see the disappointed, angry, thirty-two-year-old Biff with his American accent. Our Paul was a convincing actor! A while later, in his final year at school, Richie had great cackling fun as one of the three witches in *Macbeth*, also wonderful to see.

These nice events preceded a significant blip.

25

London 1990s business financial troubles

Tony

It was very exciting growing the business, and great to be able to give clever young people opportunities. Bob and I did our best to instil an honourable business ethos in all staff members. We encouraged them to exercise their strengths, within our ethical parameters. Bob and I were good at our jobs, but we were both reluctant to look at the broader financial picture. We were doing well, except that old chestnut, overspending, began to sap our strength. Our accountant implied that we were on shaky ground but was short on advice on how to stabilise. It was our responsibility really, as directors. We appointed an energetic new manager, but she had trouble persuading us that we didn't have the money to employ all the staff with the decent wage we paid them. We felt we couldn't part with any of them and still look after our customers satisfactorily or reduce the wages in what was becoming a very competitive field. So, we cut our directors' salaries and tried to expand the business to get more money coming in. As well as our word-of-mouth recommendations, we employed a salesman to draw in new business.

It was succeeding but we had trouble getting all the work done and fulfilling deadlines. Bob and I were working long hours, and I always wanted to be available for any GA calls, even during office hours. We were getting behind with the finances; I was starting to feel overwhelmed.

Dianne

We had stretched our small house to its limits. We upped the mortgage for the first addition to the house, a beautiful conservatory especially designed to harmonise with our house. It enlarged the kitchen, extending it into our dining area, and linked the house with the garden. We loved it and tended to live out there, with the potted kumquat and banana tree. Tom found the table nice and warm for catnaps.

Then instead of moving as the children grew, we decided on an extra floor extension, the permission dependent on keeping it in the style of the terrace. Tony had to increase the mortgage again.

I was still at art college while working for a charity that helped older people. Tony and Bob had moved the new IT business to a larger industrial space at Kensal Rise. They had bright young staff members and the business seemed to be thriving, with household names on their books. Their office had a friendly, buzzy atmosphere.

Tony was driven, always striving for perfection, but he seemed to be struggling to hold onto the various threads of his life, even with his saturation in GA philosophy. I probably wasn't paying close attention, too busy with college stuff, work, and the boys, to notice his stress levels. But he was starting to get irritable. We were busy and both of us sometimes felt aggrieved and misunderstood by the other. *What about* my *work and* my *emotional load?!* Tony could have done with a few loving hugs, but I didn't feel like it when he was tired, stressed and grumpy. We were both worried about money. I suggested lodgers, which would have been a bit claustrophobic, but Tony thought it unworkable. In retrospect, maybe I should have abandoned my studies and got a full-time job, but I was three years into the course and couldn't face giving it up – it had become too much part of my sense of self. If only one could see ahead.

One day, Tony came home pale and drained, saying we needed to talk.

'I think we have to sell the house,' he said.

I couldn't speak for a moment.

'How – did it get this bad?'

He moved closer. 'I'm sorry my love. We've been trying to muddle through. But the recession's affecting everyone. The big customers are leaving it till the last minute to pay us. And it's like getting blood out of a stone from the smaller ones. Interest rates are crippling, it all adds up.' He leaned back on the kitchen chair, 'The bank wants its money.'

I loved our little house, our home, our neighbours, our life in the street…

And our boys. How would they cope? We'd probably only be able to afford to rent a flat, not a house. How would we all deal with this? My focus became mitigating distress or trauma for the boys, and I had to hunt for somewhere local we could afford to rent. Paul was in his GCSE year, and Richie was in his final year at primary school.

It didn't take long to find a ground-floor maisonette with a small garden in a Shepherds Bush terrace. Some friends from the boys' primary school lived in a house on the same road, which was great. It was just a slightly longer trek for them to get to school. I quickly made it feel like home with our stuff, and we bought each boy a small house-warming present. They seemed all right, perhaps keeping any sadness and loss they felt to themselves; maybe they didn't want to worry us. We never heard them complain about it.

There were only two bedrooms, so we adults chose the option of the sofa bed in the living room. The boys had no power over this big change in their lives, but at least this way they had a room each.

We had read that academic decline is one indicator of emotional distress, so were grateful and delighted when Paul did brilliantly in his GCSE exams, soon after our move. Richie too showed no change in his excellent progress. Later our teenage boys went through the usual experimental antics, probably more likely due to their hormone levels and developing brains than to the loss of their home.

If we'd held on to the house, we would have been property-rich, like most of our baby-boomer friends in London; because of the crazy, exponential rise in the value of properties since the seventies. I felt like a Gam-Anon failure – guilty and ashamed – and tormented myself thinking of the often-heard advice in our group, *make sure the rent or mortgage is paid. Hold onto your home.* For the first time, I stayed away from Gam-Anon, I really couldn't face the group. Although I knew deep down there would be no judgment from any of them, I figured it wasn't a good thing to be telling hopeful new members that we'd just lost our home – not as a direct consequence of the gambling problem, but partly because of the risks my husband took with his business – his tendency to walk on a high wire without a pole. And maybe I didn't want to look.

I did use the phone to speak to a couple of Gam-Anon friends; it helped a lot to have their support. When I started going to the meetings again, everyone was wonderful and sympathetic. But for a long time afterwards, I was consumed with envy of anyone with the tiniest property of their own.

I didn't blame Tony, as I knew he had been doing his best and was distraught. Yet he had managed to pick himself up and carry on. He and Bob kept the business going.

Tony

I was still trying to run the tapestry business as well as the newer IT business with Bob. We had just moved premises to a small shop between Hammersmith and Chiswick. I spent money making it look classy, (which may have been ill-advised). I had been overstretched on the mortgage front, having extended the house as much as possible to avoid moving. Interest rates were high. There was too little ballast for the new IT business, and during the recession, the house had become collateral – then collateral damage. We were at the nadir of the nineties dip in house prices, and we couldn't even get a decent amount from the sale to pay all I owed to the bank.

It was dreadful, I felt awful. Dianne and the boys were upset and confused at first, but soon rallied, as we included the boys in discussions about the situation. Di soon recovered and leapt into house-hunting and quickly found a ground-floor flat to rent, all we could afford. But I didn't have much time to think about it as Bob and I were frantically trying to keep our business afloat. So, Dianne largely dealt with the domestic fallout from losing the house.

I felt so low at one point, that for the first time in years, I thought of escaping into the casino with its roulette wheel and bright lights. But all the years in Gamblers Anonymous paid off and I held on to the warmth and wisdom that I had found when I arrived in GA.

We had three difficult years after that. Fortunately, the GA Step meetings were my lifeblood. Each week I learned a little more about the magic of the programme. I didn't work the programme, it just happened to me. Wonderful. In fact, after those three years, when I got to our twentieth anniversary in GA and Gam-Anon, I put this in my diary:

Tuesday:

Twenty years tomorrow, I can't believe it. Spent a wonderful evening with my friends at the Step meeting. I still have verbal diarrhoea. Nothing changes. The difference in me is very real though. When Jim Taxi sent me the diary of my first four days in GA, I nearly died of embarrassment, but the garbage I was talking then is the same as the newcomer talks today. I loved the bit about owing £35. It turned out to be thousands ... so much in fact, that it was going to take ten years to pay it back. And I don't have time any more for flying model planes.

I was a hard nut to crack, my low self-esteem soon gave way to an ego of gigantic proportions, and it has taken me all of twenty years to get a reasonable balance. I am as compulsive as ever, but the programme has really got to me, and I am grateful for that.

Wednesday:

Couldn't get the secretary of Gidea Park for the person doing GA phone duty tonight but rang Tom and he agreed to do it. Di and the boys, (aged 17 and 13, both born of a non-gambling dad) are used to me being always on the phone. Big GA post this morning, a couple of sad letters. Difficult day at work, but the GA involvement puts it quickly into perspective, and I don't take my aggro home with me any more, only sometimes!

Thursday:

A day like any other. Up with the family. Off to work. Problems. Solutions. More problems. Panic ... (a new emotion that I am getting these days – I am hoping the Step meeting will sort it out for me). A quiet half-hour for lunch (well 15 minutes really). Late home after a really difficult time with a customer. Exhausted. Di home tired from work. Kids irritable. Phone doesn't stop. Gradually we all settle down. A normal day. No gambling or even the thought of it. I love it.

26

Shepherds Bush, Strand-on-the-Green, Chiswick 1990s, at the mercy of the private rented sector, friends' help

Dianne

The insecurity of the private rented sector is loathsome. After about eighteen months, the owners of our maisonette home decided they wanted to sell it. So, we had two months to find somewhere else. However, before long, with my detectorist's knack for house hunting, I found us a home in a curving terrace of tall Victorian houses linking Shepherds Bush to Kensington Olympia. The three stories were divided into spacious flats, whose populations were so transient that all our friends seemed to know someone who had lived there. Getting to school and work was a bit easier than from the maisonette.

You couldn't tell from the front of the building that the land sloped down to the railway line behind. At street level, steep concrete steps led down to our basement flat, with space enough for a small potted garden. When one walked through the long hallway into the living room at the back, French doors opened straight out onto a sizeable garden shaded by an ash tree and a poplar, with no clearly defined barrier between our garden and the next. Nestled amongst the ferns next door I spotted some familiar-looking terracotta figurines – an immediate point of connection with our new neighbour, who must have been to Jane's sculpture classes too. As I opened the back door for the first time, a striking dark-haired, brown-eyed woman came up to me with a paintbrush in her hand and a smile that lit up her face. 'Hello, I'm Mary and I'm an artist and I've got an exhibition at the Lyric!' she announced, without a pause.

Then she told us told us that our adjoining houses were owned by a private co-operative, hence the open gardens. Her side was full of beautiful ferns, and at the back was a shed she used as her studio. She was also a teacher of the Alexander Technique. Her partner, called James, was the author of a definitive book on the human voice and a published poet. They had met when James was Mary's teacher at a prestigious drama school.

Inside, their home was all rich warm colours, patterned, textured cushions, heavy fabrics, and handsome dark furniture. Mary's paintings of Charolais cows, street corners in Shepherd's Bush, and still-lifes, filled her studio, adorned all the walls in their home, lurked behind sofas, and were stacked up beside furniture. An Inuit carving in soapstone of a sea lion was one of their many lovely sculptures. A carved wooden salmon rippled above the kitchen sink.

They were friendly and kind. James was exceptionally dapper and is the only person I've ever met who had shoe lasts made for his dazzlingly shiny bespoke shoes. He always looked elegant. All of us became great friends. Later, James was my poetry mentor and even ran a poetry group for the Community Centre as one of my volunteers.

We drove our camper van to their beautiful old farmhouse in France for a few family holidays. An old barn in the large garden was set up for workshops they ran together on voice production and Alexander Technique for well-known actors and musicians. There was an ancient well in the garden that was magic – the water was so mineralised you could dip clothes in and they'd come out clean with no washing powder.

One weekend I was getting ready to make a drawing as part of my degree show. As I said before I love pelicans, the big black and white birds of Oz – I see them as symbolic of my old home. I am particularly intrigued by their awkward grooming technique, wielding those long saggy bills. I was happy to find a medieval legend about them being devoted but imperfect parents.

'Richie, will you come and take some photos of me on my bike? I need to look like I'm on the back of a pelican.' I said.

'Sure Mum, lead the way.' Younger son helpfully snapped a series of shots I could use for the self-portrait. I plastered the wall of our wide dining room hallway with Fabriano art paper and began a life-size drawing of me on the back of a pelican in flight. As I got stuck in, pastel dust went flying, the clouds gently settling to cover every surface. It seems prescient now, the resulting pastel painting of me flying off alone into a vaporous blue-greyness. I graduated from art college while we were at that flat, as Paul prepared for his A levels and made university choices.

After this landlord decided he wanted to sell our flat, Mary and James let us stay at theirs for a couple of months rent-free, as they were away in France doing actors' workshops for the summer. So we had less financial angst and more time to search for another place. We were very grateful for their kindness.

I was excited when the next place I found was a small, terraced house not far from the Thames. We were getting slicker at the process of moving. I did most of the preliminary organisation, but on the day of the move, there wasn't anyone you would want in your corner more than Tony. He had the energy of ten men.

Tony

The IT business with Bob was flourishing again, and we had many customers to keep us busy.

I was heavily involved in GA, with regular meetings and Step meetings, as well as visits to groups all over London. It was fantastic seeing people turn their lives around. I regularly helped answer the phone to gamblers in distress, or their families, and often sorted out a rota for volunteers to answer the phone 24/7, never forgetting that first phone call that had changed my life. In the early days, I was one of the few with adequate IT skills to help run the fellowship nationally. A group of us produced a monthly newsletter containing inspiring stories of recovering gamblers and their families and we organised conventions with workshops in the UK, Ireland and the USA.

There was a board set up to talk to the Home Office about compulsive gambling, trying to persuade those who rule over us of the seriousness of the problem. GA and Gam-Anon were represented; I was on it for a while and Dianne too.

We compulsive gamblers trail a wake behind us that becomes wide enough to rock families, friends, businesses, and unfortunate acquaintances. I was eternally grateful to be happy and not gambling and wanted to do all I could to help others recover.

Dianne

When we were at Strand-on-the-Green, both boys were at the same secondary school by the Thames, where they were doing well. Their time there together was brief because of the age gap, Paul was about to leave after his A-levels. The girls were a bit further ahead, finding their own successful pathways. I found it painful having to move house again, but it was fascinating to get to know another patch of West London. Despite the city's immense sprawl, each area has evolved a unique atmosphere. The vigorous, colourful diversity of Shepherds Bush links coherently with Hammersmith but is smoothed into white neutrality when it reaches leafy Chiswick. Our next home was in quiet, terraced Ernest Gardens, even further west than Chiswick, down by the Thames, a short walk from Kew Bridge by the old towpath of Strand-on-the-Green. Beside the path are idiosyncratic, elegant, eighteenth-century houses. They look as if their front doors have been made tiny for Alice's Looking Glass world. I'm assuming that for centuries, to avoid the interiors of the houses being sluiced by high tides and floods, the steps up to their doors have become ever higher, and consequently doors ever smaller. I could get off a crowded bus at Kew Bridge all hot and bothered and walk home along this path, leaving the roar of traffic behind. On the way, I'd spot herons on mooring posts or cormorants hanging out their wings to dry, while checking out the ratio of mud and water around the island called Oliver's Eyot, a refuge for Cromwell during the English Civil War.

In fine weather, customers of the three pubs sat by railings overhung with trailing willows. Their sunglasses gleamed as they chatted to their mates, while swans argued with Canada geese on the exposed mud of low tide. By halfway along I'd be smiling at people.

On weekends we could leave supper in the oven and go for a stroll to the nearest pub, The Bull's Head, for a glass of wine, to watch the sunset as trains clattered over the bridge.

My working week at the charity was four days and I had time to run art workshops with various groups: old people in sheltered housing, a group of people with learning difficulties, some children from the nearby French primary school, and a papier mâché sculpture class in a Shepherd's Bush community centre.

During the class at the home for older people, tempers flared now and then. One of the painters, a stolid, loud woman whose hearing was going, would often pass negative judgments on the work of a small, fierce bird of a woman. This poor woman had difficulty making the paintbrush work for her and even more trouble finding her words, but she had been an artist long before being afflicted by a stroke. I loved her post-stroke creations for their emotional expression and considered them more beautiful in many ways than her previous work. Not so this fellow resident and critic who had no inhibitions about mocking the smaller woman, yelling loudly, 'Look at that! What rubbish she's painting! What does she think she's doing?'

A bright flush would suffuse the victim's cheeks. She'd tremble with frustrated rage, explosive with the words she couldn't shoot back. I did all I could to smooth her ruffled feathers, but the perpetrator was pitiless and incorrigible. Sad.

Since college, I'd managed to keep up my art practice with the incentive of the odd exhibition or commission. When we lived in Ernest Gardens, I joined a local Artists at Home initiative, to produce annual exhibitions with a network of other artists. Working creatively at home, it was almost too quiet after Shepherds Bush. Apart from the squabbling sparrows in brief, silent gaps when the planes weren't going over – it was under the flight path to Heathrow – I could have been in the remotest farmhouse in Wales. The absence of human activity was disconcerting. All my neighbours seemed to be childless and away at work. When it was fine, however, I happily worked al fresco on a sculpture destined to be a standard lamp. I called the tentative embrace between a lizard standing on its hind legs and a green tree frog, (almost human in size) *Dangerous Liaison* – the first in a series of four. Once again, I was evoking wildlife in Australia, hopefully with a touch of humour.

We felt a first wrenching loss in this house when Paul left, heading for university. We drove him with all his stuff to Sussex, and after we'd dropped him off at his home share, he said, 'Well off you go then – you've served your purpose!' We laughed, happy to be dismissed.

Also in this house, the pelican-woman found a home in the garden, and our cat Tom ended up buried under the blue blossoms of a ceanothus, watered by my many tears.

We were there the year Princess Diana was killed in a car crash in Paris. The public shock skewed the world on its axis briefly; like the long-ago assassination of JFK, or Martin Luther King, and later the Twin Towers horror; leaving most of us able to recollect where we were when we heard. A friend and I trekked to Kensington Gardens to see the flower tributes for Diana and were gobsmacked by the ocean of them. The huge volume of offerings was moving, the flowers became an emotional art installation. (I couldn't help wishing people had removed the cellophane wrapping!) Diana had been a controversial figure, decidedly unlucky in love. I was an admirer of the way she used her celebrity to draw public attention to neglected issues like landmines that remain in war zones for decades after wars are finished, still killing and maiming innocents. With her kind visits to patients in hospitals with the Aids virus, she had a massive influence on changing public attitudes to be more compassionate and accepting.

Some friends with a mansion flat in Bedford Park told us they were heading back to New Zealand. Their daughter had been living there but was off to art college. These people were kind enough to offer it to us for less than its market rent. We jumped at the chance. It was the first time since we became tenants that we moved house voluntarily. The flat was on the second floor of an elegant four-storey block, spacious and charming, with high ceilings and a small balcony with room for two to sit overlooking a communal garden. Best of all it was near a tube station busy with life and people.

27

Chiswick and Shepherds Bush early 2000s, photography, Community Centre

Tony

The bedroom in the Bedford Park flat was enormous. Big enough for Dianne to section off a work area for her sculpture by the large windows facing the garden. I commandeered the second bedroom as office space after Richard left for university, with plenty of room for visitors to stay.

I loved the little night-time routine we developed. Di would be reading, propped up with a couple of pillows. She always took a book to bed, but after a day at work, she was often too tired to read more than a few pages. Within moments, the book would slip from her fingers, and there'd be the soft plop of it landing on the duvet. I'd retrieve it, remove her reading glasses, and reach across her to put them on the side table. Then, with the skill of a pick-up-sticks player, drag out the extra pillow, switch off her bedside lamp, and gently kiss her good night. Usually, she was just enough awake to thank me with a smiley grunt. A bit later, according to Di, I would sink into sleep like a log, and snore. Sometimes I'd wake in response to a gentle prod unless Di had been struggling to sleep through it when there would be a firmer one, accompanied by a sharp cry of, 'Tony!' Occasionally I would startle myself awake with a snort. Most of the time, to Di's discomfort, I managed to get to sleep despite the snoring. Eventually, she put us both on a healthy, slimming diet for a few months and the snoring became less, and my hiatus hernia magically disappeared.

For years I was troubled by nightmares. More than once, I recall trying to drive a London bus from the back of the top deck without a steering wheel. Dianne interpreted this as the frustration of attempting to run the tapestry business with my father. Spot on I'm sure, as it had been an awkward situation, with both of us exasperating the other. Those times were long gone, but that kind of dream still interrupted my sleep when I felt stressed.

When we moved to the Bedford Park flat, I was semi-retired, still a part-time director of the IT business. This freed up some time for me to indulge my passion for photography. I'd always clicked away at the family on holiday and had made a few series of the children, like video stills, to catch their expressions as they'd flit from mild resentment at being photographed to bashful giggles. I love the way the camera captures moments.

David Hockney inspired me to play with multiple images, creating montages. He explained his rationale behind the joiners. 'Human eyes tend to see various viewpoints, rather than just a moment snap-frozen in time.' I'd take many photos of my subject from slightly different angles and times. When I put them together, they seemed more than the sum of their parts. Everyone seemed to love the one that filled our kitchen wall in Bedford Park – a large picture of the skeletal West Pier in Brighton made of overlapping images.

I am fascinated by the beauty in things usually unnoticed, such as manhole covers; makers' marks in concrete blocks; and rusting locks. I try to look and see and record the intricate details of our world, as best I can.

At an Artists at Home weekend in the flat, Dianne exhibited her sculptural lamps and chickens, and I had framed photographs to complement them. We had nice, curious, genuine visitors. I loved talking to people about what inspired my photos and was chuffed by people's interest. We had a busy weekend and we both did quite well with sales. By then I was a Licentiate of the Royal Photographic Society and was working towards becoming an Associate.

Jimmy, the Director of the Community Centre in Shepherds Bush, had come to see it with his wife. He was Di's boss and had a deceptively casual, slightly shambolic air. Sweeping his arm around the expanse of his sprawling domain, he'd boast with a proud grin, 'From the cradle to the grave! We cater for everyone!'

The Community Centre is in the middle of the wealthy area where Brook Green meets Shepherds Bush. Jimmy was a clever man with a steel core and had managed to hold on to it for local people for at least two decades, despite the constantly changing political colours of the local council. He and his stunning wife Maia were Mr and Mrs Community – she worked with refugee women nearby. Maia came from the island of Montserrat but after a volcano erupted in 1995, had left along with half the population.

Jimmy's claim of service to the whole community was legitimate. The Centre was for everyone but was critically important for disadvantaged people. Newcomers to the UK with little or no English could learn the language here, but also other skills that would help them settle into London life, which can be so challenging. They could also celebrate traditional cultures from back home. There were imaginative projects to help job seekers, numeracy classes, and themed lunches to share traditional cuisines and culture. It was like a big disparate family with genuine care and compassion at its core. There were people from all over the world: Somalians and Eritreans, Ghanaians, Indians, Pakistanis and Bangladeshis, Syrians and

Iranians – quite the melting pot! Dianne worked there to recruit volunteers to help with all the services, including the project she ran to help isolated older people. I was a volunteer driver for her project and worked part time on the Centre's IT system.

A big Early Learning Centre had a nursery and parenting classes. Many teenagers of African-Caribbean origin made good use of the youth club. There was an indoor football pitch and gym. The art room and pottery were always full of students. Di's former sculpture teacher Jane taught several of them.

With Dianne and a few volunteer helpers, I drove old and disabled people for outings to London's open spaces – Hyde Park, Chiswick Park, the Wetland Centre, and so on. There were a few surprises on these outings. Those who could, came to the centre for pick-up, but some wheelchair users and others we collected from their homes. There was quite a bit of laborious fastening in and buckling down, to make safe those who couldn't get out of their chairs. If Di knew there was no café, she'd organise a picnic. Volunteer carers came for those who needed them.

Di was a stickler for training wheelchair pushers. In a role reversal, the trainee had to be pushed around in the wheelchair first; 'Now I'm going to have to tip you up to get you down the curb,' she warned, afterwards asking, 'How did it feel to be the one in the chair?'

'Erm, I'm glad I'm belted in, I felt vulnerable! And people didn't look at me when they talked, they looked at you!' Volunteers learned fast to keep people comfortable and safe.

The outings were a delight, sometimes hilarious. Most of our passengers were full of the joys of spring, appreciative of being out in London's glorious green spaces. A regular passenger, Jac, a retired actor and director, was good fun despite her numerous health issues, including a hernia the size of a football. Before the bus set off, she liked to call the register in a mock-formal voice, asking everyone to respond in her chosen language of the day. For instance, one day everyone was instructed to answer, '*Bonjour madame, je suis là*', even the stubborn one in a wheelchair would join in, smiling uncertainly, with her version, 'Bon-jua, madam, jhus-wu – what? Isn't that it?'

Nice to hear the chuckles as I drove off.

Di said the reason for that woman's frequent ill humour was because of her new state of complete dependency on carers at home. A year before she'd managed to get about, despite her amputated leg, in a three-wheeled car. A fall in her bathroom at home had resulted in a stay in hospital, and on her discharge the powers that be had withdrawn her prosthetic leg and her three-wheeled car.

Most visually impaired people appreciated someone describing what we could see in the parks, but not all of them. On one of our Hyde Park outings, where we had a lift around the park in one of the accessible electric buggy trains, a volunteer was attempting to paint a verbal picture of the Elfin Oak in Kensington Gardens for the blind man seated beside her. The commentary was overheard by a woman who didn't care for one. 'Don't you know I'm blind? I can't see anything!' she yelled. 'And I don't want to hear about it!' So prickly! But she suffered from macular degeneration. I'm guessing she didn't like to be reminded of what she'd lost since she'd worked on the production team for two highly successful TV series, *Dad's Army* and *Parkinson*. Later, however, she did approach the carved oak with the others and ran her hands over it. Sadly, I believe the Elfin Oak has since been caged.

Dianne suggested that before we rush in with help, we always ask people what sort of help they would like. Making assumptions about what we think is good for them is patronising.

Dianne

Carnival at the Centre! Our highlight of the year – a mini version of the Notting Hill Carnival. A couple of streets were cleared for the children's parade and the DJ-led revelry from a stage at the crossroads. The smell of goat curry, the rhythms of steel and samba bands, the flying feathers and beads of the dancers – so much energy. Street stalls sold food from around the world. Inside the Centre, you could make pasta from scratch with the Italian teacher of English or have your tarot cards read by the Liverpudlian education manager.

Kids leapt around on the bouncy castle wearing the faces of superheroes or butterflies painted on by volunteers. Loads of goodwill made it happen, with just a little arm twisting. I discovered early on that if you ask the right people (by which I mean those who are a good match for the job) directly and specifically, they will usually say yes. Maia's stall always made the most money as she had the knack and the charm to sell stacks of second-hand clothes. The place heaved with hordes of visitors and it always seemed to be sunny! The three local pubs approved of the carnival, as it was a great day for them.

Weeks before the event, costume makers would start being creative with sequins, scissors and glue. Our friendly Mas Band (short for masquerade) came every year without fail to help make blingy costumes for the children's parade, even though they were pressed for time with their own gorgeous costumes to make for the Notting Hill Carnival. Surrounded by children and piles of gauzy, silky fabrics spilling around the Singer sewing machines in the art room, they helped the kids make a unique little something for their costume, like a beetle or a butterfly.

Jimmy booked this regular gig with the band years before and had hooked a famous popular radio DJ who loyally came every year.

The children shone like rainforest birds with glitter and face paint and danced in the parade along the street mimicking the exuberant gyrations of the grown-ups, lithe and beautiful in sequins and feathers. Caught up in the excitement, even the shyest child jiggled around a bit.

Most nearby residents immersed themselves in the colour and fun or went out for the day. Getting the street ready at the crack of dawn and clearing all the stalls away at the end of the day, was quite the community challenge. I spent the day rushing around in a state of mild anxiety, trying to make sure everyone had what they needed. Big ladders for the bunting strung across the street from lampposts, noisy clanking sets of scaffolding poles, and brackets; then awkward six-foot-long boards and tarpaulins to cover the stalls. The first thing was appointing team leaders to put the stalls together. It made such a difference to my stress levels when Tony could help. With him in charge, about four stalls were up well before one of the others. He was systematic, efficient and energetic – it was great to have him there. Jimmy used to say that he had done a good job employing me as he got two for the price of one – Tony was a star!

At the end of the day when we were all tired out after having stood too long or rushed about all day, most of the volunteers still found the energy to wield big wooden brooms and spade the rubbish into black bags until the roads were spotless. After the noise and disruption in the middle of the leafy residential area, the street needed to be clean, so that neighbours would be supportive and complaints rare. There was only an occasional irate resident whose car had been towed away by the police because they had ignored the warning notices.

28

Bedford Park, Scottish Highlands, Venice, early 2000s, empty nest, Aussie visitor, signs of stress, magical holidays

Dianne

Tony's middle daughter, Sarah, was pregnant with her first baby when something went very wrong. She was confined to bed in the maternity hospital, lying still for weeks. Her husband stayed at our place in Bedford Park sometimes as the hospital was just down the road from us. It was boring for her and tense for everyone; but eventually, much to everyone's relief and joy, a boy arrived safely by caesarean section.

Around that time Rich set off for university in Bristol, but not before celebrating the end of his A-levels at the school ball. He dressed up as Alex, from *A Clockwork Orange*, with one false eyelash and a papier mâché codpiece, which was one of his mum's weirdest commissions!

We suffered the usual empty nest blues – the flat too quiet and sad. So it was a very welcome distraction when my youngest Aussie niece, a newly qualified doctor, came to work in hospitals in Essex and Kent for a year. She stayed with us when she had time off, and Tony was delighted to have the time to introduce her to some bucolic British icons, like Stonehenge and Avebury.

Happily for me she was around for my birthday with a zero. Tony and Maddie organised a family lunch party for me, which flowed from the kitchen into the expansive living room of the flat, with my latest big lizard and frog lamp shedding light on the proceedings. The white armchairs and blue settee were full of grown-up boys and girls and small grandchildren. The big boy uncles teased their tiny nephews. It was laughter and happy chaos with lots of wine and lovely grub provided by everyone but me!

Tony and Bob were putting heart and soul into the business, as they had in its earlier incarnation. Their company now had a board of directors with differing opinions about its future. I reckon even Jeff Bezos is not stress-free (though I could be wrong!). The two of them had always had the dream of selling the business as a going concern to enable a generous retirement package for them both. But things started looking dodgy on that front and it was of course a constant worry. Tony wasn't so relaxed at home, even a little tetchy, and at times I reacted sharply, rather than calmly. He was stressed and a bit irritable, and could have done with a cuddle, but I was too ruffled by his attitude to give him that comfort. And of course, I thought that Tony should be able to see or intuit how *I* felt, and there was no point in trying to explain because he seemed too far away. Maybe he was thinking the same. It's easy to end up on opposite sides of a divide. In retrospect, I know it's better to try and talk before hostilities escalate. We'd usually managed to talk things through before.

Eventually, in a coffee shop or over a glass of wine, we were able to loosen up a bit and make peace. We both hated living with silent tension. We talked about his work and possibly about me feeling not quite good enough – generally. Once I start, I can bawl out a list that's long, detailed, historic and pretty rubbish. Anyway, we ended up laughing and crying and closer and comfy again.

I am still friends with an Aussie housemate from the time we were young teachers in Queensland – the same salt-of-the-earth friend who had hosted our wedding do in London. She had returned to Oz years ago but was coming to Europe to celebrate her fiftieth birthday and her recovery from leukaemia twenty years before, following a successful bone marrow transplant from one of her brothers. I eagerly agreed to join her for a week of mountaineer-led walking on the Isle of Skye. I loved the idea of being out in the natural world, away from noisy London, and fancied an escape from responsibilities.

Walking in the Highlands of Scotland proved superb for clearing the brain. Up close to the sky, I could be that Aussie child again, gazing up at the mass of stars in the Milky Way, thrilled by the idea that I was but a teeny part of our incomprehensibly large universe, but somehow that was just fine. We came back enthusing endlessly to Tone. So much so, that a few months later, he also booked a scramble up some mountains in Skye. The physical effort of such a holiday was relaxing for him too. He came back much more chilled – with the proud boast that one of the Monroes he had scaled was higher than ours.

Baking his delicious bread was reducing his stress levels, as was helping lots of people in GA. He and Bob seemed to be dealing better with the financial creakiness of the business.

In winter Tony and I arranged a long weekend in Venice with our old friend Rachel. The first and only visit for Tony and me. We were charmed and Tony revelled in using his small new digital camera. Afterwards I wrote a poem, and when I saw Tony's beautiful photographs, they seemed to illustrate every verse.

La Serenissima

Some deity has crafted it –
heated it over fire and flame,
turned it in the light,
and blown art and angels
into its interior.

A pale pink tinge of a city —
trios of street lamps rosy, not amber.
Rose and sapphire glass from Murano
and the opalescent green of the water.

We watch the winter women – richly
clad in mink and fox and ocelot –
as their silvery and chestnut forms
drift in and out of galleries
glittering with objets d'art.

Gondolas slap and slap at their
moorings in royal blue rows,
vertical poles like artists' hatchings.
Gondoliers prepare to plunder the unwary
behind their gleaming C-clef prows.

We charmed lovers, winter-wrapped,
and sat on plush tapestry, gaze
at pink and pinker palaces, as our gondolier
twists his oar through the walnut fórcula
on the unswollen side of the asymmetric hull.

We float under an arching bridge
conducting tourists up, over, and down;
scrutinize a workman, laboriously hauling
a cabinet on a trolley up steep stone steps
from a boat laden with boxes.

Strings of Vivaldi melodies reach
a crescendo as we pass a concert hall.
Sparrows twitter accompaniment
from a waterside garden, its pines
susurrating in the breeze.

We glide past a sweetness of baking
– crispy galani – light-as-air,
catch whiffs of dark-roasted
espresso – frying fish –
a hint of ordure…

Back on land, we wander through endless calli,
past distressed doorways numbered in thousands,
are drawn to cathedrals of art and angels
with the heady fragrance of woody incense,
 where the touch of a button illuminates –

swirling crimson and lapis lazuli Madonnas,
walls writhing with Tintoretto, Bellini and Titian,
stone-flagged floors with tiny iron eagles
worn to simplicity and shine from centuries of tread.
We join Angelo Raffaele and San Marco gazing

across at the world's first ghetto, looking
like seven stories were crammed into five,
inhabited by Jewish merchants, moneylenders,
and physicians; until released, like doves, by Napoleon,
tearing down their island gate.

The Cimitero, on its island of Magnolia grandifloras,
tells tales of deaths too soon.
Floating above a waiting horizon
are the hazy hallucinatory Alps —
yet they seem to hug the city close.

The glass glows red when hot
and changes shape, but subtly.
The delicacy masks a sturdiness
of endurance. When cold the glittering
crystal is hard as rock, and sings.

PART THREE

2003 to 2007

Living with Illness

29

Bedford Park 2004 some tough news

Dianne

A year or so after the Venetian visit, I was late home after a busy day at the Community Centre. 'Where are you? Sorry I'm late.' I bustled into the bathroom to give Tony a hug and apologise. I rattled on about work for a moment and then noticed an unusual stillness and fullness about him. 'What?' I asked.

'I've got something to tell you', he said. A hope flickered that they'd sold the business, then died as I remembered that he went to see the doctor about a pain in his gut. 'What? What is it?'

It burst out of him with a sob, 'I've got leukaemia!'

When our GP couldn't find a muscular reason for his pain, she'd ordered blood tests with instructions to check for blood cancers. She was on the ball; it can be difficult to diagnose. The response was quick, and she called Tony back to the surgery, imparting the bad news as kindly as possible. Straight away she arranged for him to see a leading consultant, fortuitously based at a hospital on our doorstep. Bewildered, Tony left her surgery and blundered to a café nearby to try and digest the information. His afternoon was surreal. Time stood still while his mind raced fearfully in circles. *Why me, why now? Why did the world still look the same? Surely it wasn't right!* We spent that first long night in bed wide awake, holding hands, staring at the ceiling. Still as a stone knight and his lady.

Tony loved to talk, using the maximum number of words – circumlocution comes to mind. Both of us were emotional and normally had trouble not weeping, even at the mention of a kindly act amid distressing world news. The next morning, he wanted to tell everyone – his nearest and dearest that is – except for his mum, who had just lost her husband of sixty-six years. He needed their affirmation that for now, he was very much alive. He was greedy for their love.

The illness was so strange and unknown. But by looking online we began to step out of our blur of ignorance. There was so much information. The prognosis looked bleak. The avalanche of complex medical jargon threatened to hurtle us both into an emotional trough. But we mopped up each other's tears and kept within reach of a hug, or a reassuring touch. Normally I'd be driven to distraction waiting for the end of a Tony sentence, jumping in to complete it. Now I steeled myself to wait, trying to be a model of restraint. It was hard to bear his pain.

How I loved this kind, flawed hero of mine.

Seismic Fault – CML*

There's been an earthquake – the ground
just opened up and swallowed us.
More rumbling… and another shock
shoots us up amongst the ruins – barely alive –
but breathing the sweet blue air again.
Arms outstretched, we teeter along a fault line.

Are we acrobats or clowns? And who
will have the last laugh – the ringmaster?

---

* Chronic Myeloid Leukaemia

30

West London 2004 learning to live with terminal illness

Tony

Some things I simply don't understand about myself. I have a definite tendency to leave everything till the last minute, partly because I have so many fingers in so many pies. I never want to say no to anything. I probably should have rationed my GA activities at work more. I did prioritise to an extent, but I wanted to be there for gamblers in trouble. And I liked being known in GA. In fact, that's something I had to fight, the tendency to want recognition. Ironic, as GA always suggests that we are aiming for humility. I did get close eventually. But I wanted to be there for people, to be helpful. GA saves lives.

Maybe I've been addicted to a sense of danger, making my life just a bit too uncomfortable. I was driven and had a heavy workload, but I still should have made sure that certain important tasks were done, like getting my personal income tax returns in on time. Even after being reminded by my accountant, I was late and got several fines.

Relaxing wasn't a word in my lexicon. Unless it was total. I did have a reputation at home for snatching the odd daytime nap. In any case running one's own business with up to twenty well-paid staff members, including a salesman, and latterly three more shareholders, was very stressful. I was fond of my business partner

Bob but wished he would do some things differently, and I know he felt the same about me. I was never one for an easy ride and thought I could handle it, but it was at a cost to my health. I was always having gut problems and quite often back problems, probably too much time at my desk with no breaks.

I made the appointment with our GP because I thought I'd strained a muscle or something, as I had a strange pain in my gut, and I'd been waking at night drenched in sweat and felt tired. She did some blood tests and called me back to her surgery the same afternoon to tell me, gently, that she was pretty sure that I had symptoms pointing to CML, a form of leukaemia. A few days later this was confirmed by a consultant in the Haematology Department at Hammersmith Hospital.

My world collapsed. It was hard to believe in my illness when other people were going about their normal business as if nothing had happened. I needed my family and friends so much. And they didn't let me down, they were fantastic.

Dianne

The Haematology Department at the back of Hammersmith Hospital overlooks the open space of Wormwood Scrubs, where years before Tony had flown his model planes. To get to Haematology from reception one passed the ATMs and the flower shop, then turned down long corridors, passing signs indicating, 'Imaging', 'Blood Tests', even 'Peripheral Neuropathy', (I wondered about that one each time I went past – took me a long time to look it up) and on and on until we got to the department. Then we had a nervous wait on some blue seats near a few potted palms that became very familiar. Before long we were invited to a small consulting room where Professor G greeted us and gestured for us to sit down. He looked at us kindly from beneath bushy brows, his gold-rimmed specs pushed up over his thinning hair. When this doctor had started investigating CML it was incurable and pretty well untreatable. We didn't realise how lucky Tony was.

He questioned Tony in his light, clipped, precise manner:

'Has there been any change in your weight Mr Howard?'

'It's gone down in the last couple of weeks.'

'Any unusual sweating?'

'At night, I thought it was just the weather, as one does. I think it started two or three months ago and it's now a permanent feature.'

'What work are you doing, or have you done?'

'For the last twenty years, I've been in computer software and manufacturing. I'm retired and on a full salary but I'm still suffering the stress of a business in a difficult financial situation.'

'Lots of stress!' I added.

'Yes, I've never been without stress.'

I snorted a laugh, 'Tony's had lots of stress in his life. Do you think you should mention the gambling?'

'Oh yes, I was a compulsive gambler, I mean serious,' said Tony.

'What technology of gambling?'

'Roulette, casinos.'

'In London?'

'Yes.'

'Did you have a favourite?'

I laughed at the incongruity of the question.

'Yes, the Palm Beach in Mayfair.'

'Oh, my brother-in-law goes there, I've had a few meals there!' smiled the Professor.

'Ha, small world!' I said.

'But that stopped 29 years ago when I went to Gamblers Anonymous.'

'Do you have children?'

'Yes, five – two wives.'

'You don't have two wives! You have one bloody wife!' I retorted.

'How many children by the first wife?'

'Three.'

'And I think I can deduce how many in the second marriage. How long did the first marriage last?'

'Twelve years.'

'And how many years have you been married on the second occasion?'

'Thirty years.'

'And your wife is well?'

I wondered why the Professor didn't address me directly, but I answered anyway, 'As far as I know. I don't know what's lurking out there!'

'That's all one can know,' said the Professor.

'As far as I can tell Mr Howard, you do have Chronic Myeloid Leukaemia, and I'll give you a little booklet. But I'd like you to have a couple of blood tests and a bone marrow biopsy and we can confirm the diagnosis next week when I see you. Do you have private health insurance?'

'No, I'm afraid we're as poor as the proverbial church mice in terms of property and assets because I lost all that ten years ago putting money into the business.'

The Professor went on to explain the recent history of treatment and that the latest source of hope was a new drug called Imatinib or Glivec. He modestly didn't mention his crucial part in its production. He went on to say, 'Her Majesty's Government in its misguided wisdom has refused to sanction its general release yet, but the final adjudication is almost certainly that the Government will have to pay from September or October. Meanwhile, I may have to persuade someone to pay for your treatment. But – we are winning!'

He mentioned the evolution of Imatinib and the role of an American colleague Brian Druker in its development. 'It's a good story', he smiled.

Later reading more about the circumstances, we gleaned this much:

Cancer is complicated, and Tony's particular version is rare and has a unique genetic abnormality. In the 1980s a Swiss team of chemists discovered a new gene in which the head of chromosome twenty-two and the tail of chromosome nine is fused. They called it the Philadelphia chromosome. The gene contains a hyperactive protein that forces cells to divide incessantly. In 1986 the team leader, Swiss physician and biochemist Alex Matter, was joined by Nick Lydon, a biochemist from England, to look for a drug that could activate the 'off' switch in the cells. They used painstaking, repetitive trial and error to find a way of directly targeting the chromosome and developed Glivec.

But it was going to cost the huge conglomerate drug company Novartis up to two hundred million pounds to do the trials. As there were only a few thousand patients a year in America, it would not make them significant money. 'From their point of view, Glivec is a peanut. It's a small fry,' the Professor had said. Novartis eventually allowed Brian Druker a small trial with only a few grams of the product which would service a hundred patients, Druker's only chance to see if it worked. Desperate patients flocked to be guinea pigs. Very quickly their white blood cell counts dropped dramatically and became normal within weeks. Then Professor G had flown to Basel to try and persuade Novartis to produce the drug commercially, and he succeeded.

If one had to get CML – lousy idea, obviously – now was the time. Glivec promised a longer life and was a more effective and kinder treatment than the ones in general use. And one just had to pop the pills. No nasty chemotherapy. Minimal side-effects. No horrible life-threatening bone marrow transplants. It seemed promising.

Our turmoil wasn't endured alone. Tony was not one to keep things to himself, and neither was I. There was great comfort in the caring and sympathetic responses of family and friends. And soon at the hospital, we met the three specialist nurses who looked after the outpatients with blood cancers. The Dream Team. Gentle and sympathetic, funny and straightforward, they all shared three qualities you want in the face of the Big C – competence, care and compassion. With a smile, a laugh, and an unfailing willingness to mop up tears on the bad days, their empathetic care embodied great kindness. They were wonderful friends to all the patients and their relatives, which made such a difference in the long haul of cancer treatment. They were our first port of call, our calm harbour, our liaison with medical teams disrupting our lives to try and save them. Their consistent kindness over the next few bumpy years was a huge compensation for the booby prize of a terminal illness.

At the hospital, a nurse sent us off for Tony's blood tests, and then for the first bone marrow biopsy. The doctor directed Tony to lie on the bed in a foetal position. I stood next to the bed holding his hand, unfortunately with a good view of the thick needle (it put me in mind of an apple corer) in the doctor's gloved hand. Tony probably had a local anaesthetic first, then I watched as the doctor inserted this needle into his lower spine and saw Tone's face grow pink and contorted. I felt queasy, and just had time to think *Oh no, this isn't right, I'm supposed to be ...* Then I was on the floor, and could distantly hear the doctor call, 'Can someone help, please? I need help in here!' Next thing I know I am lying on the bed next to Tony's, apologising to a nurse. Standing between us she took my hand in her right hand and Tone's in her left, and said, smiling, 'There you are, I'm the conduit, now you're holding his hand!' We laughed and almost cried. I loved her for that sweet current of comfort.

That's the only time I can remember fainting.

Tony

The Professor avoided saying CML was a terminal illness and said instead that there were 'very variable prognoses for the remaining length of life'. Four to six years was the current average, but his team was leading the latest research on the newest, most effective treatments, and they were aiming for twenty and beyond.

We looked up loads of disturbing information online. Unbelievable. At times I felt desperate. But then visitors came to call. The boys, the girls, my brother and family and friends came. My daughters brought the grandchildren. How can you not live in the present with their innocent energy? 'Grandpa, what does this do? Grandpa, can we go to the park?' Just what I needed. If time was shorter, every interaction counted more. I had the wisdom of GA which I'd been absorbing for years. All vital life support to me now. *Just for today, I will live through this day only.* There was always love, always hope.

About a week after the first hospital visit, I was summoned back to Haematology for leukapheresis. Professor G had said they might keep some white cells in case I need them later. The nurses explained that in this process, they circulate all my blood and whizz it in a centrifuge to separate the cells, remove white ones, and then give me back the red cells and platelets. I said, incredulous, 'So you're taking out all my blood and putting it back again?'

'Nicer than vampires – they'd keep it!' Di said.

They put me in a reclining armchair beside a machine with two collecting bags. The bit that hurt was having a cannula put in both arms for the tubes linked to the machine and I was really a bit of a wimp. I became more stoic as the months wore on. Mind you, I was to learn that not all people who puncture your veins are phlebotomists, whose expertise would show in slickness and speed, and that some of the blood collectors must be very new to the game. After many blood extractions, finding a viable vein is like trying to win the lottery.

It was a strange sensation sitting there, with a slight, constant vibration from the machine as it hummed away, and it took hours. I had my phone, headphones and newspapers, mainly for my new enthusiasm, Sudoku. Di came with me on the bus you can hail in the street next to ours, amazingly convenient, only ten minutes to the hospital, passing Wormwood Scrubs prison on the way – it's next door to the hospital. She went off to work after seeing me settled in. Rich was home for the summer break from university, so he came in to keep me company. I was pleased as the passive inactivity was tiring, and I was tired already, a symptom of the illness. Whenever staff were around, Rich would ask them how everything worked.

It seemed hard to believe that only a week or so before, Dianne and I had travelled to Bristol for Richard's graduation ceremony. A joyful day in what was still a normal life! So glad I made it to that.

Work stress was contributing to my tiredness. Though I played a lesser role now, shortly there was the possibility of financial All or Nothing for Bob and me. We were aiming for the All, which was a secure retirement for us both and jobs for our loyal workers. IT was an increasingly competitive field, and the shareholders, of whom we had three more by then, sometimes did not see eye to eye with us directors.

31

London and Tuscany 2005, treatments, surprise flying day, a wedding, a holiday

Tony

True to his word, Professor G found funding for the trial drug from somewhere and started me on it about ten days later. I could take the tablets orally, my fatigue subsided, and in a week or so I managed to resume life as normal, (more or less). I carried on with my routines, which included sorting out phone duty rotas to make sure there was someone to answer the GA phone 24/7, doing my regular phone sessions, and going to lots of GA meetings. There were work visits too and driving for Di's Summerdaze outings. The annual carnival was imminent at the Community Centre, and I knew how much Di liked my help setting it up.

Since my diagnosis, family and friends have been making a lot of time and space in their busy lives to see me, a wonderful bonus. When I went to 'Hove Actually', near Brighton, to tell my recently widowed mother, I minimised the illness. She was in pretty good form, had taken to bridge in a big way, and was getting help with cleaning and meals. Our older son Paul was still in Brighton after graduating from Sussex Uni and saw Mum regularly, and she loved going out with him. I was also grateful that my brother was able to top up Mum's income to ensure she was comfortable and happy. She was coping amazingly well with her new status as a widow, considering she and my dad had been married sixty-six years, and he'd done all the domestic admin. My brother was helping with that too. He's a good man; I am immensely proud of him and his success.

A day came when I couldn't go to a concert as I felt too ill, the drug was making me nauseous. The medics gave me something to counteract the nausea. The following week I had a few days with muscle pain and night sweats and was worried about being well enough to attend a friend's wedding on the South Bank. Di and I loved it there, London *is* the Thames – the history of generations of creative minds is palpable. The bride and her husband were both actors at a theatre in Ealing famous for the quality of its amateur productions. We were to watch a daytime performance of *A Midsummer Night's Dream* at the Globe, celebrating our friends having tied the knot at a register office earlier. Our party was to stand up in the middle, like the proletariat in Shakespeare's day. My daughter Sarah and her husband were friends of the bride too.

'Tony, I could only find this director's chair – you'll be able to direct proceedings!' my son-in-law announced. I accepted gratefully as standing for that long would have done me in.

It was a great performance, and the bride and groom were overjoyed. Outside the theatre, the choppy Thames sparkled to the clinking of moored boats.

In the following weeks, the illness made its presence known from time to time, in muscle and bone pain mainly at night, but otherwise I was able to function and enjoy whatever I was doing. Dianne organised an amazing birthday present for me. When I was nineteen, I'd learned to fly in a de Havilland Tiger Moth biplane. Knowing this, and my love of everything aerial, Di organised a family picnic at a small airfield near Windsor. The adults all had a chance to fly. The plane was a beautifully preserved red Tiger Moth. The pilot flew at first, but once airborne he would relinquish control to any willing co-pilot sitting in the bucket seat in front. I was thrilled at the idea, but just a little worried about fatigue and my ability to cope with all the excitement.

We found some grass near the small runway and children and picnic hampers were unpacked. They insisted that I went for the first flight, and my son-in-law began filming.

There was a one-size-fits-all leather jacket. 'Actually, it's two sizes', the pilot grinned, 'too big or too small!' It fitted me well however, and I zipped it up firmly and hauled the leather helmet with a microphone attached over my ears, goggles perched above and beamed at my family ranged before me on the grass. I paused for photo ops, clambered into the front seat and buckled up. As I looked up at those familiar wing struts, the years fell away.

The other guy in attendance reached for the top of the single propeller and flicked it down hard. The plane shuddered, spluttering into its lawnmower throb. As it warmed up the young man moved to wait near the blocked wheel. 'Chocks away!', the pilot yelled, and his mate kicked the block away and gave us the thumbs up. (I was delighted they still said that!) We chugged along the small runway, pausing for our turn to take off; then the pilot hauled the stick back, we gathered speed and lifted off sharply away from the earth. It was so familiar – wind in my face, the noise, as the fields and roads below shrank to map size. We flew around in a loop and the pilot tilted the plane so I could wave to the family briefly below. Then he handed me the controls. Wonderful!

Everyone who flew that day was brave enough to take control, my daughters, my sons, Dianne; and it was fun watching everyone's antics with the grandchildren from my camp chair. What a fabulous day!

I needed regular hospital checks to monitor my progress on the drug. It seemed to be going well, my white cell counts were going down. Sometimes an unpleasant side-effect would turn up, and the medical team would do their best to sort it out. I was starting to make friends in the waiting room at haematology. I was so lucky to live close to this teaching hospital, some patients had to travel from the Midlands or even further.

I don't remember talking with Dianne about squeezing as much as possible into our lives, but that's what we seemed to be doing. Hospital and GP appointments were interspersed with lovely events. Even the hospital visits were spiced up with the company of friends or family. A few weeks after the flying day we went off to Italy to meet up with Di's sister and brother-in-law from Australia.

Dianne

None of us had visited Florence before. We'd arranged to meet Anna and Jack in the Piazzale Michelangelo, where there was a car park with the best view in the world. (I believe cars are not allowed to park there any more.) We were there first and walked around the bronze cast of Michelangelo's David and stood on the terrace, gazing out at our god's eye view of Florence. Under the generous expanse of Italian blue sky, we could pick out the octagonal red cupola of the Duomo, the tall bell tower of Badia Fiorantini, and caught a glimpse of the Ponte Vecchio over the Arno, tucked within the honeycomb of the elegant sandstone city.

Anna and Jack were coming from Rome. 'G'day Di! Tony!' they called as they arrived, and we rushed to embrace one another and weep a little. Nothing like spending most of your lives apart to make you aware of how precious the time is with loved ones from far away – even more amazing in the splendour that is Italy.

After exploring Florence at ground level, we set off to find the Tuscan villa we'd hired, where Anna and Jack's second daughter and her boyfriend were joining us. When we'd established our territories and settled in, Paul started imparting the rudiments of Wing Tsun to Rich. It's a Chinese martial art. I have photos of them facing each other under the shady portico, arms extended, eyes locked, serious.

In the heat outside, the indifferent olive trees ran downhill in straggly lines. On every local road were Tuscan men on foot, with every male over the age of fifteen toting a rifle, maybe looking for birds to shoot, as you could hear the *pock-pock* of distant gunfire nearly all the time.

We couldn't get over the Rightness of the beautiful way Italians built cities on hilltops. From one of the towers of San Gimignano, we marvelled at the clusters of medieval sandstone houses below, the spaghetti network of narrow streets, and endless blue-green valleys beyond.

I loved the meshing and melding of my Oz and UK families, even though parting was always heartbreaking, especially now Tony was so ill.

32

London, Australia 2004–6, Alexander Technique, business failure, struggle to earn money, great holiday

Tony

I felt all right a lot of the time, but there were side effects from the drugs, a price one had to pay to stay alive. Alexander Technique seemed to help, so I was going to Shepherds Bush a couple of times a week for lessons with our old neighbour and friend Mary.

'Tony, can you just stand here, in front of the stool? I don't want you to do anything, except when I ask you to. Just leave everything to me,' she explained on my first visit. In her workroom were a stool and a table to lie on. It seemed I had to surrender physical control of my movement to her, which felt amazingly relaxing. Mary went on talking, explaining all the while what she was doing, instructing me to stand up and sit down with her hand supporting my neck, like a gentle puppet master. Then she told me to lie on my back on the table with my knees drawn up, and she put a couple of books under my neck, selected from the large collection on the shelves behind. It was a strange feeling of submission as she took hold of my hand or bent my leg, adjusting their positions slightly, finding what was right for me and, I suppose, the pull of gravity. I could feel a big difference after she'd lifted my shoulder gently and smoothed it down. No tension, no jarring. A pleasant absence of trying – a letting-go.

As I explained to Di later, it made me feel more fluid, and lighter. I was more relaxed than I had been for years. Mary had said it was a way to be kinder to yourself in everyday living. I was struck by the similarity to the GA message of Letting Go.

I was using my diary to record things then.

2004:
Health Summary:

Cramps – all minor only.

Fatigue – slows me down after a couple of hours of activity – need to sleep afternoons where possible. Tend to pig out in front of the box until 1 am, don't like it.

Food – quality not bad but eat too much.

Back – always near to pain if I bend or twist knees, noticeable when standing from sitting. Using Alexander Technique all the time – good.

August '04:
We had a shareholder's meeting in June when Bob had produced a budget plan, which we thought would save the day. Since then, the business has been through administration and purchased by a rival instead of a staff buyout. So now I have no income, no shareholding, and have to get income again.

Di and I did our arithmetic which showed that with a bit of paring down, we can pay expenses but not enough to eat as well! I have two viable options: 1) from photography and 2) from computer networking support. Both can produce some income – I need to always be planning on methods that are self-supporting so that they are not simply based on my sale/support time. Rupert, our photographer friend, introduced me to Andrea who seems keen to be an agent to sell pictures to restaurants, etc. If it works, I can seek out agents in other areas e.g. Islington, Campden, Hampstead etc. Needs good tight budgeting. Selling greeting cards will be good too if I can recruit someone to do the rounds of the shops. This needs pre-packed stock that's quick and easy to display – and priced to be the middle between cheap and dear. Always unusual images and interesting packaging. Fixed selling prices including VAT and 50 per cent for shop. Had a period of feeling wakeful all day, but this seems to have reverted to being very tired by 2 pm and needing to sleep.

Dianne

My poor Tone. The last material citadel had crashed. It was finished. The outcome that he and Bob had hoped for, dreamed of, had always been working towards, was a comfortable retirement for both. Not to be. It was a considerable setback, particularly given Tony's state of health, and age – so close to retirement. He was upset of course, but not destroyed. He took an admirably pragmatic approach to what he could do next.

I didn't understand exactly. Their business seemed to be flourishing. Bob and Tony made sure that each customer's IT system was neatly tailored for them with nothing extraneous and was as user-friendly and foolproof as possible. There were household names on their books. How could a business full of clever people with such a nice friendly working environment and a rather noble business ethos, be considered worthless? If that's what being 'under administration' means.

But hey, I did know that neither Tony nor Bob liked dealing with the money side of the business, I guess therein was the fatal flaw. If only they'd had a decent, tough, business manager.

When it was in administration, all the staff members, apart from the two who had approached the rival company, put in their own money to try and buy it, but were outbid by a hostile takeover. I found out recently from Bob that all the staff went on to success elsewhere.

At that stage of Tony's illness though, it was just another negative to negotiate. I hadn't really expected the most optimistic outcome, and I still had a job and even minuscule savings. It was an added stress for both of us, but the important thing now was Tony's quality of life. And we knew how to live one day at a time.

At the Community Centre, Jimmy was looking for a reliable person to provide support for their IT network, and he was delighted to employ Tony part-time. Tony also took on some private clients with PC problems, while continuing to develop his photography business. He still did a huge amount of work for GA, of course. We planned to show our artwork together at the summer Open Studios event, his photographs with my sculptures. He was still my favourite volunteer driver for the Summerdaze outings, and he planned to help again at our children's carnival. He wanted to tackle tasks with the same gusto, but tired earlier, and I worried about his slightly dodgy back.

One of my Aussie nieces was getting married that year, so, believe it or not, the day after his birthday that September, Tony and I boarded a plane bound for Oz. We had help with the fares from my kind family who were keen to see Tony, and we could stay with them as well. As presents for everyone, he took some of his photographs printed on canvas.

We flew to Perth first to stay with my cousin and his partner on their farm in Denmark, south of Perth. They gave us a self-contained cottage with an eco-friendly floor of rammed earth. (I called it eco-friendly; our hostess apologetically called it 'primitive'.) The cottage was overshadowed by a forest of karris, huge hardwood eucalyptus only found in this southwest corner of West Australia. 'Beautiful,' I said. 'I hate them,' our hostess replied. I can't remember exactly why. Maybe partly because they are extremely tall and inflammable. Must have been scary in the face of bushfires.

The animals in Oz are quiet, but the birds are loud. I grinned with delight to hear the wonderful melodic warbling of the Australian magpie, which looks more like a black-and-white crow than a UK magpie. Cockatoos and rainbow lorikeets screeched noisily all around us. There was the odd kookaburra who came to laugh, and each morning before dawn I was woken by a bird that I named the 'Ethical bird' – exhorting me, apparently, to, 'Give Eth a call – she'll do the washing up!' (Repeated endlessly in case I didn't get the message.) Unfortunately, I was never able to establish the whereabouts of Eth, to help with the washing-up!

We hired a car to tour the Margaret River area, famous for its wine. One place we stayed was a rambling old farmhouse with a treehouse feel. An enormous deck was covered by a branching network of marri trees, like eucalyptus. One evening our superb chef-hostess Siobhan and her Tuscan husband made delectable thin pizzas in the domed, alfresco oven. We were invited to wrap them around smoky eggplant, (aubergine), peppers, and feta. Cicadas chorused fortissimo to pianissimo and back, while a baby possum stared at us with huge glass eyes mirroring the fairy lights on the veranda, clinging tightly to her mother's furry back as she climbed up the rough red trunk of a marri. Dried leaves underfoot released a hint of eucalyptus, and our hosts' orphaned pet joey, Bellissimo, loped over to us, hoping for leftovers. Tony succumbed to the appeal in her doe-like eyes, and she ate fragments from his proffered palm, clasping his hand gently with both her small bony paws, ending in big black claws.

Tony was in his element, filling reels of film with photos of honeyeaters' long beaks in the spidery red flowers of *Grevillea*; huge termite mounds amongst trees; ancient Aboriginal fish traps of low stone walls in a sheltered inlet (indicated with explanatory signs); floating and flying black and white pelicans, and frothy red or yellow gum tree flowers.

We made our grateful goodbyes when we got back at my cousin's place, before flying off to New South Wales to visit two nieces in Sydney.

One was in a sandstone terraced house with lacy ironwork. We wandered with her around the harbour, enjoying its expanse of sea and sun – the sailboats, the Opera House, and the bridge, just like a Ken Done painting. We saw a black cloud of fruit bats at dusk, setting off from the park to feed.

It was wonderful to see the girls and catch up with their lives. Unfortunately, while we were enjoying a tour of the home of an iconic Australian artist, Tony's back suddenly 'went', with a spasm of agony and immobility. He crawled out of the predicament with pain killers (praise be!) and remembered his Alexander lessons.

At work in Shepherds Bush, I had been lucky to have enlisted the service of an Aussie volunteer while her husband was working in London. She'd enjoyed making regular visits to an old person in her home, to ease her loneliness. The couple had returned to Oz, and when I told her of our visit, she and her husband generously invited us to stay on their property north-west of Sydney. It was on the side of a hill overlooking rolling pastoral country a bit like Devon. Once again, we had a place to ourselves, this time in a cabin made of parts of an old shearing shed.

I sketched Tone staring at the Akubra cattleman's hat in his lap trying to work out what to do with the leather strap. He has a look

Point Lookout, Stradbroke 25/10/04

of intense concentration. I think the drug was giving him a bit of brain fog, and his back was hurting …

Thence to Queensland to see the rest of my lovely family and to the wedding. Afterwards, a whole lot of us went with the bride and groom to Stradbroke Island, not far off the coast of Brisbane – yes, while the bride and groom were on their honeymoon, but not staying in the same place. Straddie had been a favourite holiday place of Anna and Jack's family of four girls throughout their childhoods.

My old mate had come to join us on the island for the day, and we were enjoying a blissful swim in the warm waters of Cylinder Bay. 'It's like molten glass,' she said. Later we wandered around the headland and saw dolphins surfing in the waves. Tony was restricted to the veranda of the chalet, as his back was hurting too much to walk around. But he said he was happy with his cushioned sundowner chair and a low teak table laden with drinks and puzzles. He could sweep his binoculars over the bay to try and spot dolphins and whales.

Tony

Back in Blighty again, I was adding to my diary entries:

I am having a difficult time preparing for an Artists at Home weekend – frustration dreams again. One of them included me having my credit card in my pocket which I did not lose or leave behind on my frustration trail! Suggesting, ironically, that money is not a worry!

My dear daughters clubbed together to pay for a birthday break for Di and me which was brilliant! A welcome long weekend in a hotel in Wales overlooking a lake. I remember drinking a glass of bubbly while bathing in bubbles!

I'm realising I must make 'end' plans. Not just will and funeral but talking to responsible people to take over my roles. I am having trouble deciding what to let go, as I still want to do all that I am capable of. But neither do I want to let anyone down.

33

Chiswick 2005 another health event, moving again, the joy of nature, a wedding

Dianne

Tony phoned me at work, but his voice was so weak I could hardly make out what he was saying. He whispered, 'Pain, I can't ...'

I rang for an ambulance and grabbed a colleague whose car I could see parked out the front.

'Peter, can you please drive me home right now? Tony sounds dreadful.'

He did so without question, which was good of him as we hardly ever saw eye-to-eye at work. We arrived just after the ambulance, in time to open the door. Paramedics are some of the nicest people. They reassured Tony, gently manoeuvred him into a wheelchair, and then lugged him manfully down four flights of stairs. I clambered into the ambulance too and it set off towards Accident and Emergency at the nearest hospital, Hammersmith, the one treating his leukaemia.

The doctor on duty in A&E was puzzled about the source of his pain. He tried an enema which just caused Tony more distress. Later another doctor just coming on shift thought it was most likely a burst diverticulum on his colon, meaning urgent action was

Back in Charing Cross 19th Dec 05
7 5th floor bar (looking North)

Fulham Palace Rd

needed. This hospital had only a minimal provision for surgery, and they'd have to get him to Charing Cross fast. He was bundled back into another ambulance.

The driver did his best to inch over the speed bumps gently on the way out of the hospital grounds, but Tony winced at each impact. Reaching the road the driver accelerated with blue lights flashing and siren on. Inside the ambulance you could hardly hear it, it seemed nothing to do with us. Thankfully when we reached the hospital a surgical team was ready and waiting for him. My heart contracted as I kissed his furrowed brow before they whisked him off to the operating theatre.

This life-threatening incident was unrelated to his cancer. It hardly seemed fair.

During the operation, they hoovered up the poison leaking into his body cavity, removed a section of his bowel, and made a stoma in his abdomen. So now he had to learn to live with a colostomy bag, something we would all want to avoid. During his recovery in hospital, he learned how to manage his stoma and poo bag with the help of a specialist nurse. He was discharged into a network of support from a brilliant team of district nurses, and he learned to cope quickly. Mostly they would just supervise while he changed his bag, cleaning the area scrupulously.

Tony

I was shocked to wake up to a bag covering a hole in my gut. I had taken my alimentary canal for granted, as you do, assuming it would last me a lifetime. However, I was grateful to have survived and thankful to the medical professionals. The stoma nurse helped a lot in the hospital and when I got used to it, I found it wasn't that bad living with a colostomy bag. Also, it wasn't expected to be permanent. The surgeon said that they should be able to reverse it in the future.

At some point later the drug Glivec stopped working for me, and I went downhill. But once again I was lucky as there was another trial of a slightly different drug that worked in a similarly targeted way, and I was eligible for that too. And this new one did the trick, stopping my body from over-manufacturing white blood cells, thank goodness.

The year progressed much the same as the one before. I was getting on with bits of money-making work while making plans to wind down major commitments, as my current prognosis was not that promising. I was feeling tired, and my concentration was going a bit. The love and care shown by friends and family made me very aware of what was most significant in my life, and I felt very fortunate. But there was a wound from the operation near the stoma site where some infection had begun and it wasn't going away, despite my careful cleaning.

It was a shock when our friendly landlord told us that she wanted to sell the flat in Bedford Park. I didn't want to lose our comfortable and convenient home. Although, as my last visit to the hospital demonstrated, it was difficult for paramedics to manage four flights of stairs without a lift. I found the stairs tiring too, though it was good exercise. But I didn't much fancy going through the disruption of moving house again. I'm sure I was irritable. Dianne found it a blow too – we loved breakfast on our little balcony, the happy memories of family gatherings around the kitchen table, and having a comfortable spare room for the boys when they came to stay. However, Di was off house-hunting again and soon found an upstairs maisonette not far away. One flight of stairs, a great improvement, opposite a park with a little playground – great for visiting grandchildren. When working from home it was so much nicer to be able to see activity from the windows. Not at all grand, like Bedford Park, but a couple of very pleasant terraces of Edwardian maisonettes, all with some garden front and back, many with mature privet hedges like ours. It lacked the vast floor space of the mansion flat, but there was plenty of room and a back staircase reached a private little garden area. Di asked the new landlords to remove the tumbledown shed before we moved in. They were helpful and cooperative. The flat was even closer to the hospital bus for the regular clinic check-ups and within walking distance of the tube station. It was accessible but quiet, away from main roads. With all the palaver of address changing yet again, it's a wonder our friends bothered to keep up! But they did.

Di was quick at transforming places so within five minutes it looked welcoming, cosy, and beautiful as if we had been there for years. We had a sofa bed in the living room for visiting family. One of the bedrooms was ridiculously small but useful as a storage area for my many files and tools. There was a box room at the front which I used as an office, with a view of the park. While at my desk I could look down to see birds darting in and out of the privet hedge – robins, dunnocks, blackbirds, and even an occasional wren. Di put up a bird feeder by a back window which attracted noisy starlings, who pecked one another with their needle beaks. Blackbirds sang away in the plane trees in the park, especially after rain. Dianne found a back route through Ravenscourt Park to cycle to work in Shepherds Bush or walk if she'd allowed enough time.

By this time, I had built a website for my photographs and started adding a health blog as well. I was recovering, but everything took a bit more effort. I was just about able to provide IT network support at the centre. I was working on some writing to add to GA literature and enjoying the GA Sep meetings where we had practical and philosophical discussions on life after gambling.

Kind friends gave me lifts to and from the clinic for my regular visits, some even stayed to keep me company. Family and friends, knowing Di was at work, were giving me their time, company, and love, which was quite delightful, and made me value my life even more.

After discovering the Wetland Centre in Barnes on one of Di's Summerdaze outings, I started catching a bus there whenever I could. Redundant reservoirs had been reclaimed as habitats for water birds and for humans to enjoy observing them. I loved the tranquillity of the reed beds and took great pleasure concealing myself in the hides, watching birds preening and feeding. I was thrilled by a flash of blue and orange as a kingfisher darted by. Otters played by a bank in the sun. I was learning to identify ducks – a favourite was the male Mandarin – so splendid in his oriental garb.

Another favourite haunt was Kew Gardens, so I took myself off there often. It was even nicer with the company of friends or family when they were able. Camera at the ready, I strolled among the trees, with half an eye out for goose poo, as the Canada geese are prolific in every way. Kew Gardens is a great place to observe small seasonal changes and it was a favourite weekend hangout with Di. I took my best photo of a robin there.

That year my youngest daughter, Ava, looking radiantly happy and beautiful with her equally happy and proud new husband, had a lovely wedding celebration in Central London, which I managed to get to with Di and the boys. The newlyweds went off on an exciting, protracted, globe-trotting honeymoon.

34

West London 2006 in and out of HDU at Charing Cross Hospital

Dianne

I look up as we stop, and three boys from Latymer Upper School enter the train with their blue and grey ties loosened at the collar. They all seemed to have teeth braces and talked about their last class as they found their seats. I thought of my boys having similar conversations when they went to that school, (without the braces.) These boys had divided opinions. I glance at the copper clock as the train pulls away. The Roman numerals indicate quarter to four. I wonder idly if primary school children could read the time on it.

It's gloomy outside and the train's getting crowded. The end window of the carriage is open a crack, and I have claimed an armrest; but a man has just lowered himself heavily into the seat beside me, wafting an odour of *I'm a real man who doesn't wear poncy deodorants.* I whisk my arm away and edge towards the glass divider. I'm washed by a wave of sadness, almost grief. The same kind of exhaustion that relieves an athlete of self-consciousness enables me to relax into the sadness, and I don't try to hide it. The woman sitting opposite me has thick curly black hair tumbling over her narrow gold specs. She eyes me perceptively from her iPod sound wall and looks as if she might be about to ask if I'm all right. So, I look her in the eye from my brimming ones and give a little grin and nod, which probably looks odd.

We're moving again and mini diamond rivers form on the window outside. There's a weird greenish light – the trees have a backdrop of pewter but the sun glistens on their wet trunks and the leaves glow bright green. Gusts of wind cause more flurries of tree rain. Soon I'll be home, after a welcome wet walk; I'm equipped for it, and it will be great to have a little exercise in the open after the hot sterile atmosphere of the hospital.

We're at my stop, Stamford Brook. It's a Victorian platform with bargeboards edging the roof like picket fencing. Once again, I'm at the wrong end of the platform and must walk a hundred yards, but I don't mind, more walking is good. As I slap my purse on the Oyster disc and the barrier arm moves, I am pleased with the ease of this way of paying while registering that I need a top-up.

Maybe my expression still looks open from the exhaustion of hospital vigils, for people in the street glance at me in a friendly way and smile. This is London, isn't it? Or could it be that my mascara's running with the tears and rain, giving me panda eyes – I'm too tired to care.

I feel no guilt at leaving the hospital early today, as my younger son came late and can stay a couple more hours in HDU with his dad. I'm sorry for our sons, with the strain of it all; but having them around has been amazing. Richard has just graduated from Bristol, and his brother Paul is travelling up and down from Brighton on the cheap coach between work shifts. They make the situation bearable. They are wonderfully kind to their sick dad and me and make us laugh. And both have been doing some fantastic cooking. Last night there were slices of grilled aubergine with a tomato salsa topping; followed by vegetarian pasta pungent with garlic, extra virgin olive oil, and parmesan shavings. And tonight, there is reliably yummy 'Jewish penicillin' (chicken soup) left by my kind sister-in-law. So once again no cooking! It's a relief, as the last few days have been draining.

The staff in the High Dependency Unit are kind and efficient with patients, and patient with their relatives. From the broad windows of A Bay at HDU (if you are upright), you can see an amazing panorama of central London. The Post Office Tower, the Albert Hall and Memorial, St Paul's Cathedral, Canary Wharf, The Eye, Big Ben, Westminster Cathedral. Inside this ward, the air-con hums, monitors click, and Tony's nebulizer hisses. Nurses and visitors chatter, a radio talks quietly, a patient moans, the phone rings; the doorbell buzzes, and someone laughs. The yellow clinical waste bin closes with a bang. Why, when those identical-looking ordinary waste bins can close silently?

We've had a few anxious days with Tony in hospital for another operation which was not due to his CML. It had been elective surgery, but there was a mishap afterwards.

Following surgery the year before, there was an entry wound a couple of inches from his stoma which was expected to heal up normally. Unfortunately, that wound had become infected, and the infection had grown. Over months, infected tissue, a fistula, grew from organ to organ. This latest round of surgery was to remove the infection and reverse the colostomy at the same time. However, as the operation proved tricky and took a long time, they decided it was too risky to change the colostomy arrangement.

We were waiting ages for him to be brought down from the recovery ward after the surgery, but when his bed approached, they wheeled it right past us, and there was an air of consternation. When I was allowed near him, he was barely conscious but murmured, 'Morphine …', which he normally hated as he reacted badly to it. I touched his tight-looking belly and it was hard as iron. An artery had burst after the operation and was bleeding into his gut. They couldn't give him pain relief as he had to be rushed back to the operating theatre.

He moaned again as I stood by, helpless, desperate for him to be knocked out and pain-free. He was surrounded by nurses managing drips and bags of blood. With *ER*-type urgency, one nurse named Rhea directed people to move Tony's bed to the operating theatre to staunch the blood. But in the corridor, they stopped, waiting for – something. Frustrated by this, she yelled, in a broad Aussie accent, 'Have we got an anaesthetist or am I doing this on my own?'

A gowned medic appeared, and they wheeled Tony away fast. But Rhea called over her shoulder that she'd be back soon to tell us what was happening. True to her word she returned twenty minutes later to say, 'Look, he could be dozens of hours. You might as well go home. Someone will phone when he's out of theatre. Don't worry mate, he's got the best surgeon.'

The Christmas break of another on-call surgeon had been interrupted for the second operation. Since we lived only ten minutes away through night-time traffic, Richie and I went home, shattered. Just before midnight the surgeon phoned to say they had stopped the bleeding, and all was well and that they would keep him in Recovery overnight for blood transfusions and observations. Relieved, we went to bed and slept.

The next day at the hospital, however, our patient is agitated. He says, 'You're on the wrong side!' We move to the other side. A nurse comes to the Wrong Side to do a procedure. His agitation increases and his legs tremble, 'No, no, go back, you're on the Wrong Side. You don't understand!' Apparently if we cross a line between curtain rail and window, we cause him terrible pain. A doctor comes to the rescue with an anti-narcotic drug. Gradually the agitation is less. His imaginings are so malevolent. It's sad that his hallucinations aren't more pleasant. If he's going to be brain-jiggled with morphine, it's a pity he's not having fun. Later, however, his fancies improved and became more benign. Apparently, this was taking place on Hammersmith Station: (he'd written it down somehow!)

They toggle (sic) *over from flour to grain. With a brush it switches –
and the cost is the same – the press of a button or a switch. And they're
sorting out the meat over there, I can hear them!*

Later, while he was drifting in and out of this vivid alternative
world, with plenty of medical supervision, his younger son gave
him this simple joke to fasten onto: 'What's yellow and invisible?'

He paused, pointing into space, 'Those bananas!'

This proved very difficult for Tony's befuddled brain but kept
him busy all night and freer of imagined darkness. With a bemused
grin, he tried to recall it: 'What's orange and you can't see it?'

Then tried, 'What's over there and yellow?'

Many more permutations and combinations were employed
until he was exhausted and fell asleep, no doubt much to the relief
of the poor staff and any conscious fellow patients, who were all
familiar with the concept, if not the joke itself, by the handover the
next morning.

Out the hospital window Charing Cross Jun '06

35

London 2006/07 hospitals and drugs, Wetlands, Kew Gardens, Shaldon, the Highlands

Tony

After that operation, I spent a lot of time in hospitals, and check-ups at the clinic dominated the gaps between visits. There was pain and distress of various messy kinds, and the medics realised in March that the current drug I was on for my leukaemia had stopped working. Then they put me back on the first one, and a month later another new one. Bit of a roller coaster. I tried to deal with the various pains and discomforts without being too much of a burden to everyone. I felt tired a lot of the time. Di was managing to get to work, with help from her very understanding boss; no problem with flexible hours, and friends and family were there for me with visits, sometimes with gifts of food, and always with love. Any day I felt reasonably well was a joy.

Humour reliably lightened my mood, as in this text exchange with Paul:

Me: Are you enjoying your gift for art?
Paul: You sent a gift?
Me: No.
Paul: I'm using my gift for retorts.
Me: Gas fired?

I'm happy in an elemental way but sad too. I receive so much kindness from health professionals and often from strangers. Music is a lifeline. I often play Arvo Pärt's *Spiegel im Spiegel,* for the melancholy conversation between piano and cello – so serenely hypnotic and beautiful. I think I would like it at my funeral. I have an insatiable appetite for watching the musical *Chorus Line,* there's something about the endless repetition of the percussive song and dance routines that I find oddly reassuring. Now that my days are numbered, I seem to want repetition – I'm not resistant to it like the weatherman Phil Connors in *Groundhog Day.*

Mobility scooters are great for propelling myself around Kew Gardens and Barnes Wetlands, though I often need help to get there now. It's great having friends for company, but also good to have an element of independence. I can trundle or whizz around the paths at my own pace, spotting waterbirds on the ponds or listening to blackbirds in the trees and enjoying a coffee. Even at Kew's bridge-like Alpine House, I can drive in on the mobility scooter to take photographs of tiny unfolding plants in their tiered rock garden beds.

There are weeks when I feel much more normal, and during one of these Di and I popped off to Devon for a few days. We got the pedestrian-only ferry from the beach in Teignmouth across the river mouth to Shaldon. Its length of service is mind-boggling; it dates from the thirteenth century and has a black and white livery. The ferryman told us the 'gunports' were painted on after the Napoleonic wars, to make the ferries look like fearsome men o'war. What a history in passengers, over so many journeys.

Sheltered by the red sandstone cliff of Ness (made green with the trees planted on top by order of Queen Victoria) at Shaldon, I sat on a bench with my tea in typical British Old Person fashion, though still not identifying as such. I faced the busy bay, watching big container vessels coming and going at the port of Teignmouth across the water. Before me, there was so much colour and life. A clinking cluster of small sailing boats was at anchor with children racing from beach to sea – splashing and shouting around them.

1903 & 1909 Sealit2 Shaldon - Teignmouth   Aug '06

Teignmouth Dock – busy! Aug '06

Shaldon Beach '06

The bench was my go-to spot when I wasn't feeling up to a trek with Di. We had tried walking up the Ness together one day and I got about halfway before I felt breathless, and my legs hurt. So I happily watched people enjoying themselves on the beach while Di went off for a more vigorous walk by herself.

Back home I can still do phone duty for GA, but I'm trying to let go of more demanding jobs, though I don't want to let people down by leaving things undone. Dianne reckons I'm too hard on myself. Lately, I've been remembering what I was like when I first turned up at GA. When I think back on the terrible qualities I showed then – the big ego, arrogance, conceit, super sensitivity, lying, and wrong decision-making – I realise I have made *some* progress over the years. I've done my best to help others by retelling my awful backstory again and again, which is how GA works. I explain how much better I feel since stopping gambling and tackling normal life. I'm able to face all its challenges head-on and deal with them. I know I have contributed to keeping the wheels of the fellowship turning.

Even if I can't always sustain it, I manage a little meditation and come closer to serenity more often. I have learned much from the decent behaviour of people around me, and from my ongoing efforts to apply the wisdom of GA to my life. If life gives you a knock you've no choice but to recover from the blow and get on with it. Acceptance is crucial and is not the same as complacency. Action is required to do what you can about any given situation constructively and realistically. I have learned to count my blessings daily – and there are many. I'm much better at appreciating life from moment to moment. I've almost learned to go a little easier on myself – because I need kindness too.

Some GA friends set up a few meetings at home when I wasn't well enough to get out. At the most recent one, lots of my oldest friends in the fellowship came, and each recalled incidents when they said I had helped them when they were at a low point. They were still rude enough to make me laugh, but loving and complimentary. It was emotional, almost overwhelming.

I've always loved planning holiday breaks for us. I like looking at maps and plotting journeys, working out where to stay and what to do. We were still trying to snatch the odd weekend away.

The Guggenheim Museum in Bilbao had been a hit with both of us. We both loved the building, it reminded us of the Opera House in Sydney, and Di had been shocked to discover that she loved Jeff Koons' huge Puppy sculpture outside the museum, as she usually loathed his work. It was beautifully planted with alpines. When it comes to artwork, my Dianne has strong likes and dislikes.

Since we'd both enjoyed our separate Scottish holidays a few years before, I had been concentrating on organising a Highland break for us together, travelling by train to the highest mainline station in the UK, Corrour. It's near Loch Ossian, and accessible only by train or foot. There was a restaurant and a place to stay there. But as the date got closer my health went into a dip, and I knew I wouldn't be able to manage it. I was about to cancel, when Di said, 'Hang on, I could do with a break. What if I get some people to keep you company – Tony-sitters?'

'Absolutely, great idea! It's only a long weekend,' I said.

In no time I was set up. Both sons, a friend with an outrageous sense of humour, Emily, and my brother and sister-in-law all agreed to come and keep me company in shifts over the weekend. I looked forward to a comfortable and light-hearted time with them all. But we had to find a friend for Di – someone who could use my Senior Railcard concessionary tickets.

Dianne

I found the perfect candidate for Tony's tickets. She was quietly and practically generous, eagle-eyed about what needed doing, offering low-key help, always with a touch of humour. Our friend Ann had just got herself a Senior Railcard and was available that weekend. It was nice to show her our gratitude, and good for me to have a congenial travel companion who was also an artist.

It had been exhausting looking after Tony and working. A week or so earlier I had acquired a Macmillan nurse overnight as Tony had been confused for a few nights and I'd had very little sleep. She kept an eye on Tony while I slept. Those nurses are amazing.

I was disappointed and sad that Tony was not well enough for Scotland, but despite a twinge of guilt, excited at the prospect of an away break. I knew he was in safe hands and he would have fun – within his current parameters of fun.

Travelling up the coast by train, then walking in that sublime landscape with sky and weather and great grub and wine and company, was wonderful. Ann and I trudged up to a steep summit – only to find another ahead of us and another. But then stood with the wind in our faces gazing across at a theatre of mountains – smoky clouds curling round peaks – speedy curtain calls obscuring the sun for seconds at a time – light – shadow – blue – bright – dark – feeling close to the gods and utterly privileged. The air was so pure and clean.

We had excellent meals; one of venison with onion jam and neeps and tatties. We reckoned our charming, earthy hostess was a superwoman who shot the deer in the morning, butchered it, cooked the venison, nipped out to fix the engine of their Land Rover, did all the domestic chores, and still had the energy to be nice to all the guests at mealtimes. We weren't sure what was left for her husband and son to do.

I dislike hunting and shooting and fishing normally, and hardly ever eat meat but will still occasionally eat venison if the deer is likely to have been killed in its ideal environment by an invisible hunter with a single, accurate shot. I see this as the least bad exploitation of animals.

Before we left, Ann kindly bought me a mug I'd admired from their gift shop, decorated with an excellent drawing of the station house and a stag, which I still think of fondly as a gift from Tone, indirectly. When we got back, people kept asking me where I had been because I looked ten years younger! A good prescription for carers – escape to the Highlands!

36

London 2007 wheeling
Tony in parks, kind people

Dianne

One of the district nurses organised a wheelchair for Tony, as his legs had become too painful to walk on. He could just about manage the stairs, slowly. It was sad unfolding the wheelchair at the bottom of the stairs for my formerly robust partner. People gave us sympathetic looks as I wheeled him around the park opposite the flat. One day we came across a friendly young family; one of the daughters had acted in a community play with Tony. 'Hi Tony', Niamh said cheerily, 'Where are you off to?' And she introduced us to her mum and sisters. It was great for Tone that she talked to him directly in the chair, as we found it was common for people to address me, the pusher, the upright one apparently in charge, reminiscent of the Radio 4 programme *Does He Take Sugar?* The moment you sit in a wheelchair people tend to assume your brain has gone to mush, or they simply don't see you.

The play had been part of a community drama week at the Lyric Hammersmith. It was inspired after Niamh met actor-director Jac at the Community Centre by chance and they immediately clicked and became firm friends, closing the generation gap. After some discussion, we set up an intergenerational drama project. Older people told children stories from their lives and the children interpreted them on stage, with help and coaching from Jac and another couple of volunteers. Tony recounted an incident when he'd travelled to Norway as an unaccompanied child of about nine, to stay with an uncle and aunt. He and his cousin had been making 'music' in the kitchen with saucepans and implements, when the father came striding in, his face grim and pale, as they were bashing a battered old pan. He snatched the pan from their hands, saying in an icy tone, 'No! Not that one!' The children were frozen and intimidated, but Tony found out later that the pan was the only vessel the couple had used for every conceivable purpose in Auschwitz.

Our latest neighbourhood had been familiar to us for decades. It wasn't far from the house where the boys grew up. I could take Tony from our local small park through quiet back streets to Ravenscourt Park, and usually come across old friends who talked to us in a normal way, even if some of them had trouble disguising their sorrow or pity.

One sunny afternoon Tony struggled down the back stairs to our garden where I had put a bowl of elderflower punch on the table with mint and big dark cherries floating on it. He sat facing a wrought iron arch thick with honeysuckle and the flowers of a deep blue clematis. From the centre dangled a mobile made of delicate shells and sticks from Stradbroke Island, where we had had such a lovely family time together in Oz. The niece who had stayed with us in Bedford Park had made it as a memento. It was accompanied by three defiantly flying pigs. Tony wore a Panama shading his rimless glasses. His green eyes looked large and beautiful in his slimmed-down face. The face that was so gentle now. He was so good at appreciating the joy of moments. The friend who accompanied me on the Scottish weekend, Ann, joined us. Robins and blue tits were flitting and singing, it was an enchanting couple of hours.

I just wanted him to be happy and comfortable to distract him from the hurt of the dreadful disease, and to have as many moments like this as possible. The bastard illness seemed to be taking over, causing him pain that the painkillers could not entirely obliterate, especially in his legs.

37

London 2007 small comforts, gentleness

Dianne

It's not one of his better days. He sits with his feet on the low tapestry-covered stool, Thai silk rug snugly around his legs. A fresh cup of green tea is on a Japanese coaster on the adjacent glass tabletop. An oval silver pot waits with its divided contents: two large yellow capsules of Imatinib, and the agglomeration of drugs for supper time contained in the opposite curve. His leg jerks and he can't suppress a small yelp of pain. I offer to warm a barley bag in the microwave. It soothes the pain, a little.

Sandalwood smoke drifts in from the bedroom as a Schubert piano sonata rises and falls, and he struggles to keep his eyes open. But he wants to see the golden light illuminating the plane tree in the park opposite, dramatic against the steely sky, and whatever's happening underneath the tree.

Despite the smell of imminent rain and the rustling of leaves, a man plays basketball with his son. The dad can't resist grabbing the ball from the boy's grasp and hurling it up to the net beneath the tree – a hole-in-one. The boy bends forward in mock despair, head in hands. A younger boy makes a frenzied circle pumping the pedals on his mini bicycle with stabilisers, irritating his brother trying to retrieve the ball. Tony looks with enjoyment at the flashing red lights of the little boy's trainers and the glossy curls flicked back from the older boy's face as he focuses on aiming for the net.

But Tony's eyelids are getting heavy. 'Shall I read a bit of ' *Tis*? I ask. 'Mm', he agrees, and I sit on the floor by his legs on a cushion. We've been enjoying this cozy companionship as I read aloud from Frank McCourt's memoir. I'm not attempting the accent but trying to get the lilt of the text. It's quite an emotional journey, one moment I'm doubled up with laughter, making Tony grin, the next halted by a sad passage, momentarily unable to speak.

As I resume the story, I glance up at him gazing at me, his face open and gentle. 'I love watching your face change when you read,' he says.

CML* Spring

> White snowdrops
> > furrowed brow.
> Blue and yellow crocuses
> > eyes with blue shadows.
> Yellow daffodils on greens
> > pain across his shoulders.
> Pink clusters of cherry blossoms
> > on his tummy a rash appears.
> Starbursts of creamy magnolia
> > the pain has company – diarrhoea.
> Chestnut candles – light on dark
> > nausea now, but the rash is less.
> Yellow forsythia spikes into gardens
> > activity is shortened by fatigue.
> Orange-yellow Easter roses
> > a restful night, with pain reduced.
> Bright green euphorbia with bluebells
> > he greets the morning with a smile!

---

* Chronic Myeloid Leukaemia

38

London 2007 hospital, home, hospice, distress

Dianne

In July Tony was once again an inpatient at Hammersmith hospital. His immune system had taken a huge knock coping with the last operation, which would be why he caught MRSA and on the next visit, Clostridium difficile – both infections rife in hospitals at the time. Given their virulence and his weakened state, it was amazing that he recovered.

When he got home it gradually dawned on us, and his physicians, that the current drug he was on for CML was losing out against the cancer cells in his body. Nights were becoming chaotic with his pain, twitching, confusion and distress.

I followed the complex regime of drug administration to the letter, but it was hard for medical professionals to get the dose right to keep the pain at bay and not cause him distress or delirium. The doses needed constant tweaking by specialist medicos. One night he wanted to get up for a pee but couldn't work out what to do, even though I was doing my best to help.

Like most humans, my natural urge is to try to relieve the suffering of anyone in front of me. In that situation, I assume a practical and straightforward mode and keep my churning stresses till later. But I was having trouble coping with his torment. He needed someone there all the time, and I was still trying to work while he was in and

out of the hospital. It looked as if the medical team would not be able to pull him back from what could be the end stage.

When not being a nurse, I was in a tizz about everything. *How long will his suffering go on? Can I keep my job? I'm barely holding the project together. how am I going to pay the rent on my own? How am I going to manage? What else can I do to help him?*

At work, I was not as efficient as I was at home. I felt like a dragonfly darting here and there, except a dragonfly has more of a sense of purpose! Thank goodness for my understanding boss when I was in flibbertigibbet mode.

Even so, it wasn't all terrible. There were periods of respite when the pain was at bay. Tony glowed with the love of visiting friends and family, and there were many moments of levity. Like when he was asking me about his tablets at Medication Time:

'What's that one?' he asked.

'Citalopram.'

'What is it?'

'Umm ... a mood lightener.'

'If you had it upside down it'd be a mood *swing.*'

I laughed. 'Good one Tone.'

I wrote this in my morning pages:

Thinking about Tony and death is making me nervous and tired. Certainly, I don't want him to suffer any more, he's had enough suffering for a thousand lifetimes. Whatever is to come next it doesn't look good.

I haven't had much time to feel, too busy looking after. You're fading away before my eyes, my love, getting thinner, whether you manage to eat or not. You had been such a fidget in bed, legs or arms twitching or jerking. Now it's easy to lie peacefully beside you, with the new stillness. Except for the shuffles out of bed for a pee, or to empty the bag, or the whimpering of pain if it's been too long since the last painkillers. You're too bony and insubstantial to cuddle. You wince if I try. You are slipping away from me slowly, so slowly.

I miss your skills – so clever on the computer, and so conscientious about finding the best way. Where did this stubborn tenacity come from? Your resilience? Your spectacular ability to recover – till now.

One day when you were in hospital it seemed so empty and silent at home. I got a glimpse of what my future would be like – and got all bereft and gloomy and negative – lost, really.

Can't project though, only deal with the now as well as I can. One old friend from France talked to me sympathetically about the burden on 'my tiny shoulders'. He made me chortle ... 'tiny shoulders' indeed!

These are my notes after another hospital visit, and a discussion with his surgeon and cancer consultant:

The prognosis is still weeks or months.
The leukaemia will not kill him, it will be an infection or a bleed.
His body is more susceptible to infection and increasingly weaker.
He can come back here to this ward or go to Pembridge hospice to sort out his pain relief as necessary.
The surgeon is in favour of him returning to this ward in the hospital as they all know him.
The other doctor is in favour of Pembridge as all the doctors are pain relief specialists.
A multi-disciplinary team will look at his scan results and decide whether further investigation or treatment is necessary.
If Tony wished, they would stop life-prolonging treatments.

Pembridge was the nearest hospice, behind St Charles Hospital, off Ladbroke Grove. It aimed to provide sensitive care and support for chronically ill people or those close to the end of their lives.

39

London 2007 life in the hospice

Dianne

Pembridge felt tranquil. The areas for inpatients were ground level and spacious, with French doors often open for fresh air. There were only a few people in each ward and some single rooms. For outpatients, and any inpatients who felt up to it, a nearby block housed a whole lot of activities.

For patients and their families, there was a bright conservatory with facilities for tea, coffee and Wi-Fi, with a large kitchen table and chairs. People were often in there with laptops and books. Volunteer actors visited periodically to read for patients who were too ill to do it themselves. There was a relative's bedroom for overnight stays, but I ended up sleeping in Tony's room sometimes. The ratio of nurses and doctors to patients was generous. We were to find that all the staff had kindness written through their cores like Brighton rock.

On our first visit, bemused, we saw a couple of smokers with their beds and drip trolleys half out of the French doors so they could have another fag! *Well, I guess it hardly matters now,* I thought.

When things became too much at home, Tony was able to have several short stays at Pembridge, rather than in a hospital. Before I forgot what the palliative care consultant had been telling me to explain Tony's pain, I made these notes at the hospice:

The pressure of too many white blood cells causes the pain. The bone marrow will grow in places it hasn't since he was a child.

Arms, legs, breastbone. The chest pains could be caused by bone marrow trying to grow in the ribcage.

Oh God!

But it can subside as well. When Tony showed signs of too much painkiller – toxicity – manifesting in e.g. paranoia, hand tremor and confusion at not being able to pick up his glasses with one hand; they whipped off his morphine patches and said they would replace them with a lower dose. It wasn't because of the oxygen as he's had hardly any today.

The consultant said that he's particularly sensitive to painkillers and that slight variations can make a big difference. Their effect can change from day to day, depending on what else is happening. He seemed to have peaks and troughs, and that in trying to allow for the peaks, the dose was too much for the troughs, hence the dose reduction.

Poor Tone, it goes on and on.

We spent Paul's thirtieth birthday having lunch in the conservatory at Pembridge, all the family together at the long table. It was lovely, but I hope our boy got to go out in the evening with friends.

Around Tony's bed I'd pinned an assortment of pics of his nearest and dearest and a few beautiful photos of flowers he had taken in Kew Gardens. Plants and flowers were allowed in the ward, (unlike hospitals) and the girls had given him gorgeous pots of purple and white Cymbidium orchids, and there were loads of cards from friends and family arranged on all available surfaces or stuck on the walls. Home from home. Interesting how easy it is to create one's territory. Like camping. He didn't like being alone so there was a constant stream of visitors when I was at work.

In the conservatory, said a wobbly note on Tony's pillow, the day I was meeting Graham, Hannah and Rebecca for their first visit to the hospice. As I approached with brother-in-law, his wife and daughter in tow, Tony's face lit up. They were frequent visitors after that. We seemed to spend a lot of time eating when they were there. Hannah always brought tasty tempting snacks, or one of us went out in search of something comforting and delicious, like bagels with cream cheese and smoked salmon or even sugary doughnuts. Tone's visitors weren't getting any thinner. Otherwise, we tried to 'help' Hannah with crossword clues – though she almost always got there first; or we'd read or have desultory conversations with the patient when he was awake – slipping in and out of time. Occasional chuckles broke the quiet. It was gut-wrenchingly sad but also warm and comfortable. We were there together because we loved him.

I was writing out my distress in 'morning pages' – reams of barely decipherable scrawl in my blue fountain pen:

Tony's intellectual capacity is diminished by drugs and illness. He's been shedding his body like a snake sloughing off skin after skin. There are horrible nodules hurting his bones. He cries out in pain when they wash him. Human touch hurts him now. How long will his suffering go on and how long can I cope and how will I cope afterwards, as well??

I was outside Pembridge having a breather one beautiful blue evening, when I heard a great whooshing, and a pair of swans flew low over my head. Joy. For life, and beyond…

40

Pembridge London 2007, the boys say goodbye

Dianne

Tony was sharing a small ward with another man in Pembridge. Members of the other patient's family were around a lot of the time, so there were murmurings and comings and goings. Tony always liked me near him now, even at night. On one of these nights, I was sleeping in the chair beside his bed when I was roused by the rasping of curtains, then a light coming on, a scraping of chairs and a scurry of activity. In the morning the neighbour's bed was empty.

We absorbed the implication with mild shock, but I was relieved for my Tone's sake at the silence and peace, though it didn't half underline the reality of his situation. I went out to find the deceased man's family. They were at reception looking stricken and pale, and I stumblingly offered our condolences.

The staff didn't plan to put another patient in the room with Tony. We had him to ourselves in privacy, which was much better. But I knew he'd rather be at home when he died. With a little trepidation, (thinking how difficult it was to care for him when he was confused with drugs and illness) I sought the consultant's advice when she next came round. 'Do you think it would be possible to arrange for Tony to have a hospital bed at home?'

'Well,' she said, 'that takes about a week to organise; I think perhaps you should be telling people to come and see him this week …'

It had been creeping up on us for weeks now, but it was still a jolt to realise it would happen – soon Tony wouldn't be with us ever again. It was getting so close to the end. I was shattered from still trying to cover my job at the centre while not getting much sleep. On autopilot I made phone calls and sent many texts, and everyone responded. I enlisted the boys' help I think, and arranged a rota of visitors that week, allowing gaps for rests. Much as Tone loved to see people, the effort of attempting social interaction exhausted him. Of course, visitors preferred to make their farewells when he was awake and verbal, but he was spending more time asleep and eating and drinking less.

My boss Jimmy had said kindly, 'Take all the time you need Dianne.' So I stayed at the hospice, since Tony had made it clear he preferred me with him all the time. The children managed to be there a lot too. Many old friends came to see him, speaking compassionately and quietly of their fond memories and love for him, whether he was awake or not. We needed a fair few tissues.

From my 'morning pages':

Tone seems to have developed pneumonia – he has a phlegmy cough – which at least will provide some lubrication for his throat – if he doesn't get choked by it – has to cough it up occasionally. Honestly, would we let ill animals suffer like this? Why poor human beings that we love? Hope the children realise how proud their dad is of them. Almost said 'was.' This transitional period of even worse illness is cruel. Why, oh why? Why all the suffering? Buddhists would tell me, no doubt, rationalising the human condition. There are so many ways of doing this …

How long does our poor Tony have to endure? Please Good Orderly Direction, or whoever you are, can you see your way to releasing my poor husband, father of boys and girls, brother to two? Could you not let the poor man float away peacefully, comfortably? He has had enough pain and suffering.

Quite a disturbed night with the throat, the mouth, and the coughing. Anyway, the mouthwash fixed the halitosis – but I can't bear it – can't bear not being able to give him water. It's awful to see his mouth clamp down on the little sponge meant to moisten his lips – he tries to suck it.

The day before his birthday we were all more or less camping there – Graham, Hannah, and Becca, Paul, Richard, and me, with Naomi, Sarah, Ava and many friends popping in and out when they could. There were birthday cards, texts, and emails to tell him about. The girls all made their emotional, individual farewells. We were doing Hannah's crosswords, eating continuously – strangely enough; being a bit silly, staring into space if we felt like it, and comforting one another.

Rich wrote this message in my notebook:

I want to talk to you before I talk to Dad. I want to tell him what a wonderful dad and a wonderful friend and a wonderful teacher he has been, and that all we have for him is love, and I want to tell him that it is OK if he wants to go …

We had a sad but lovely day together, and Graham, Hannah, and Becca didn't go home till late.

I'd started making a list of stuff we might need the next day. Tony seemed restless and uncomfortable again though not conscious. A doctor increased the dose of morphine in the syringe driver to ease his pain. We understood from discussions at the hospice that dying people can probably still hear. Tony's breathing began to slow, and we spoke to him of our love.

The boys told him:

'I remember sitting on your shoulders and pulling your eyebrows up.'

'I remember being carried half-asleep from the van to bed.'

'You've been a great dad; I don't remember you ever being mean to me.'

'You never expected us to conform.'

'We loved that cheesy naan you made under the grill in the camper.'

'You've instilled in me your fascination with everything – with all creation.'

'Whatever choices I made I felt supported.'

'I'm sorry I was such a surly adolescent.'

'You were a lovely dad who told me often that you loved me.'

Then Paul collapsed in tears, sobbing, 'I don't want you to go, Daddy!' Richie and I hugged him. Then, for a while, we all sat or wandered, tired and dazed, listening to Tony's laboured breathing. There was another change when Richie went out to the conservatory to phone someone. A nurse came in to check on Tony and told us gently that it wouldn't be long now, so I went to fetch Rich back. Dear Tone was lying on his side. His eyes were open but unseeing, and I had to move behind him, away from his eyes. Our two sons and I held him gently in our arms and talked to him. 'We're all here with you my darling …We love you … It's okay, you can fly away now … Good-bye … We love you …'

As he finally exhaled, we seemed to see his soul leave his broken body.

Our beloved Tony died an hour before midnight. The next day would have been his birthday.

I found I could call my Tony 'Darling,' as the flesh shrank from his bones. As he was hardly able to hear, my endearments became 'my darling', and 'my beautiful man.' Why couldn't I have found it easier to call him 'Darling' all our married life? Don't quite know, really.

The nurses said there had been a nice feeling in the room and that Tony would have known he was wrapped in love at the end.

Paul, Rich and I held one another, sniffling. We were relieved that he was no longer in pain, but felt heavy, not quite knowing what to do next. Paul was very emotional and could hardly put one foot in front of the other. Rich coped by thinking practically and being busy. I was a bit unhinged, exhausted but brisk. None of us feel the need to sit protectively near the body that had betrayed Tony with its nasty pains and nodules. We broke the news to the rest of the family and Graham Hannah and Becca came back to the hospice. We all cried again then fumbled our belongings together and they drove us home.

When they left, we opened a bottle of wine. Paul gave an emotional toast, 'To Dad, who knew what was important.'

41

London 2007 joyous farewell, comfort of loved ones

Dianne

The boys had to go back to their own lives soon. I phoned my sister in Australia and told her I needed her.

Jewish funerals still happen fast. Graham was keen for us to follow that tradition. Tony died on a Thursday, and we managed to arrange the funeral for the following Tuesday, with the help of an excellent funeral director in Ladbroke Grove that I had already approached. We went to see him together, the boys and me. He was very tall and very kind. 'Tell me about Tony,' said Mr J, suggesting we call him Robin. We told him about GA, photography and bread making, and that he always found time to help people. The boys said what a great dad he was. Robin scribbled away on his notebook with a fountain pen. I said it would be nice to have some of the feeling of a big, happy GA meeting. 'Some people have told me already they are willing to give a eulogy,' I said, 'though I find that word a bit cold. I'd like people to be able to talk about anything they remember about him – doesn't need to be praise – if it's affectionate, and I think we can guarantee that.'

'Sounds good,' said Robin, 'You can approach this however you like.'

We wanted a secular service, humanist in style, but we were all happy to have some religious input from Graham and Naomi,

Sarah and Ava, who had been brought up in their mother's more traditionally Jewish household. We wanted Robin to pull it all together. And music – music was important – though I didn't find Tony's note about *Spiegel im Spiegel* till too late, so I hope he forgives me that it wasn't played. We planned some readings from favourite texts of ours.

Thanks to the afternoon on Acton Green with Becca and the pelican wings, we surprised people with the cover of the order of service, using the photo of white wings extending from Tony's dark jumper, making him into a relaxed, urban angel.

We booked a double slot at the crematorium to allow enough time to celebrate Tony – his last party – although he wouldn't be there (would he?). As my last gift to him, I wanted a natural-looking pile of flowers tumbling over his coffin. The florist did not disappoint.

I didn't like the idea of people feeling obliged to spend lots of money on floral tributes that are then thrown away, so we asked all the guests to bring a single bloom to hold during the service. It was quite magical to see people with their flowers. The sun shone on Tone's Day. Loads of friends came, some with their grown-up children. Many were from GA and Gam-Anon. Jimmy had arranged for two busloads of people from work. Family and extended family were there. My Aussie niece Lou came from her home in Bangkok for a few days to join us – leaving her new baby behind and having to use a breast pump daily!

I felt emotional but happy with all my family around, greeting and hugging our guests. The chapel started playing the Schubert Piano Sonata no 21 in B flat, which Tony had loved, and people drifted into the chapel. As it began to overflow, some headed upstairs to the gallery, which filled up, so a few had to stand. Most mourners remembered to bring a flower. Some of the Jewish men found it disconcerting, as Jewish funerals are normally plain and unadorned. The coffin was already on the green marble catafalque. A glory of purple wolfsbane, pink roses and gerberas, creamy freesias and globes of green hydrangea rested on top, with eucalyptus and ivy cascading aromatically over the sides. So beautiful. Sun strobed through the stained glass and stroked the freesias.

Our tall funeral director was even more imposing, resplendent in top hat, tails and embroidered waistcoat, exuding a great sense of occasion. He welcomed everyone, beginning with, 'Life was Tony's religion, and his focus was on living life to the full.' Everything he said about Tony was warm, human and relevant. He invited Paul to light a candle and some incense.

Becca was first with her tribute. She had been tearful earlier but now was composed and eloquent. She talked about her uncle's influence on her photography. 'I like to feel that I have internalised his way of seeing – to look at something not for what it might obviously represent but for how it presents itself to me uniquely at any given moment. I never spoke to him about this, but I wonder if he might agree that is how we should regard each other in life. To look beyond the outward appearance of what we think we see and examine from different angles the things that make us who we are; good, bad and ugly, which we might eventually reassemble into a different whole viewed with new eyes.'

Each family member walked up to place a rosebud and a small stone on the coffin. Then Dave, the National Secretary for GA, spoke about the work Tony did over decades, and how he had helped thousands of other gamblers and their families. My boss Jimmy talked fondly about how much he had done for the Centre as a staff member and as a brilliant volunteer. Naomi and Ava read from the Forms of Prayer for Jewish Worship.

In the middle we had Jessye Norman singing 'Beim Schlafengehen', by Richard Strauss from a poem by Herman Hesse. This was to enable me to sob and howl, (so to speak, within the constraints of being Anglo-Saxon in origin and being in public) and to provide a space for everyone to feel their losses.

Then we had our actor friend Jac read the first part of Dylan Thomas's, *Under Milk Wood*:

> 'To begin at the beginning: It is spring, moonless night in the small town, starless and bible-black, the cobblestreets silent and the hunched courters'-and-rabbits' wood limping invisible down to the slow, black, crowblack, fishingboatbobbing sea. The houses are blind as moles ...'

Love it! We'd loved it together. And then Jac said things she liked about Tony and called him 'a very elegant gentleman.' Rich read a favourite of mine, a short poem by W B Yeats:

> He Wishes for the Cloths of Heaven.
>
> Had I the heavens' embroidered cloths,
> Enwrought with golden and silver light,
> The blue and the dim and the dark cloths
> Of night and light and the half-light,
> I would spread the cloths under your feet:
> But I, being poor, have only my dreams;
> I have spread my dreams under your feet;
> Tread softly because you tread on my dreams.

Graham then delivered his eulogy, likening his brother's life to a game of football with two halves, the better half being the second, as he recovered from gambling. Then he read the Jewish prayer known as The Mourner's Kaddish, explaining that Tony had read it when each of their parents died, and he thought Tony would appreciate it.

GA believes gamblers, with help, can stop their gambling but are never cured. So, Bill, a long-time friend and fellow traveller in GA, made this announcement causing a few chuckles. It almost named this book: 'Tony is now Officially Cured of gambling!' And then continued his light-hearted tribute. A couple of other friends bravely went up to the front to deliver fond memories, and then everyone recited the Serenity Prayer:

> *God grant me the serenity*
> *to accept the things I cannot change,*
> *courage to change the things I can*
> *and wisdom to know the difference.*

Paul read this Joyce Grenfell poem:

> *If I should go before the rest of you,*
> *break not a flower nor inscribe a stone.*
> *Nor, when I'm gone, speak in a Sunday voice*
> *but be the usual selves that I have known.*
> *Weep if you must,*
> *parting is hell.*
> *But life goes on*
> *so sing as well.*

Then Robin rounded it up with, 'May you find comfort and richness and example in your memories of Tony. May you find support in your love for each other.' Then he reminded everyone they were invited to the Wetlands Centre in Barnes because Tony had whiled away many peaceful hours there. As they were leaving, mourners placed their flowers in a large basket. Afterwards, we took the glorious basket of colour to Pembridge for staff and patients.

Graham and Hannah very kindly paid for the funeral, so I was able to pay for the flowers and the Wetlands Centre. Mourners were invited to donate to Pembridge or Leukaemia Research. We hoped to scatter his ashes in an avenue he had photographed on a misty day at the Royal Botanic Gardens, Kew.

Ella Fitzgerald and Louis Armstrong gave us an upbeat farewell at the end with 'They Can't Take That Away from Me.' We both loved Ella and Louis.

A few days later I had this note from Sarah:

'The service yesterday could not have been bettered. I would say it was the most excellent memorial service I have ever been to – it had Tony's hand and yours – and I'm sure Paul and Richard's hands written all over it! Simply beautifully done! It must have touched the hearts of everyone there – it certainly did mine. It was a delight to have 'They Can't Take That Away From Me' ringing in our ears at the end of the Service.

'I really don't have to tell you what Tony meant to us both. I always felt so secure in the knowledge that not only could I talk to him about anything – but if I had a concern – or a problem – he would be there to discuss it with. We both loved and respected him, and now feel quite bereft that he is no longer there.'

And from another old friend:

'…The ceremony had an extraordinary immediacy. We were all able to fix Tony in our minds. He was conjured up so beautifully. When your MC alluded to the coffin being hidden, I spoke to the guy next to me, who was in GA. He said what I was thinking, 'I'd forgotten Tony wasn't here!' What we were both feeling was that it was difficult to grasp that he wasn't there, as he had been so vividly brought to mind in that chapel. It was a jolt to remember that vivid memories are now all we have. You and Tony had each other for less time than you would have hoped for. But it was long enough to create a double act that others looked on with respect and admiration.'

Thanks to Rebecca, many still have the photo of winged Tony on display, all these years later.

After the service, most people made their way with us to the wetlands in Barnes.

42

London 2007 at Barnes Wetlands, animals, birds and people comforts

Dianne

It was sunny, and the glass wall of the Observatory made the interior a cathedral of light. Outside the reeds rustled and mallards pottered about. We had photos on display – some that Tony had taken and more of the family. Next to them was the overflowing basket of sunflowers, lilies and roses that we later took to Pembridge. It was heart-warming to have all these lovely people coming together to celebrate Tony's life. One of 'my' volunteers at the service was a photographer, who took snaps of people placing their flowers on the pile in the basket on their way out of the chapel' and many pics of the mourners at the observatory from a balcony above them. In the photos, everyone looks quietly calm and content. People were either standing talking to old friends, sitting together with their excellent coffees, or contemplating the view outside – as Tony had done.

Several things concerning animals or birds gained significance in a most comforting way. I'm hardly the first to imagine soul transference to other creatures after the death of someone close. I felt that Tony was keeping a benevolent eye on his loved ones to make sure we were okay.

The first was a big ginger tomcat in the Wetlands car park. I hadn't exactly been a mad-about-cats-woman since our Tom died, but this cat came straight up to me, reminding me so much of Tom that I immediately picked him up and draped him over my shoulder, as I used to do with Tom at bedtime. He stayed there like a sack of potatoes and purred like a lawnmower, exactly as our Tom had done. It *was* Tom! Or it certainly seemed like a sign from Tony.

The next day, Ann and I took my sister to Sloane Square to have coffee at the top of the Peter Jones store. We sat beside a large window with a view of sky, rooftops and London icons, like the Brompton Oratory dome. It isn't an area commonly known for water birds. But just as our coffees arrived, right next to our window was a heron – magnificent wings slowly beating, legs trailing. Glorious. Another sign. It reminded me of when Tony lay dying at Pembridge, and a pair of swans flew low over my head, wings humming.

Robins have become symbolic of Tony in our family. He was fond of them and had taken quite a few pics, and one turned up in Kew Gardens singing his heart out in a shrub next to the *Poliothyrsis sinensis* where we gathered to scatter Tony's ashes. (I had requested permission, and we went to our spot with an official escort before the gardens opened to the public.) We found the small grassy avenue between the trees where Tony had taken a misty morning photograph.

The robin sang away, not even taking flight as we took turns awkwardly spooning out the ashes, which are more like sandy grit, around the roots of the oriental tree. It's also opposite the Tree of Heaven, so he has a nice view.

Near Tony's tree, appropriately, there was a sculpture by Emily Young called 'Wounded Angel.' The sculptor is reverential of the material she carves. On her plaque, the only information was about the geological origin of the stone. I took the liberty of placing the heart-shaped stone I had put on the coffin, at the base of her plinth.

Tony's tree still thrives.

I'm more agnostic than atheist, and willing to embrace a bit of magic about the marvellous unknown. Our friend Jac, who read from *Under Milkwood* at the funeral, had written Tony a warm letter about feathers and guardian angels. Thinking of this much later, and prompted by a writer friend who had meant to say, 'weather forecast', but said 'feather forecast', I wrote this poem:

Feather Forecast

Ethereal wings may quiver
over the earth - discarding
a white feather or two,
spiralling
    gently
    downwards
for someone in need
of a guardian angel

– predicted a friend,
when one I loved
was very ill.

Feathers in my path
everywhere,
after he died.

Warm curls of comfort.

I was happy to assume that it was Tony offering reassurance and comfort; I never worried about the actual origin of the feathers.

After the Wetlands, we delivered the beautiful basket of flowers to Pembridge and got home worn out and hungry from our emotional day. It was a wonderful surprise when a piping hot, fragrant goat curry turned up on our doorstep, home-cooked and hand-delivered by Maia and Jimmy – so thoughtful and kind.

43

London 2007 hanging out with Sis, speedboat on the Solent, empty flat

Dianne

It had been a joy to see my niece Lou, but after the funeral, she needed to get back to her baby and husband in Bangkok. Thankfully Anna could stay for the rest of the time I was off work. She was keen to provide me with a comforting luxury and bought me two big downy pillows. Together we tackled Tony's clothes, her practicality was welcome for such an emotional task. We put aside his two nice towelling dressing gowns for the boys to wrap themselves in, and I wore his pyjamas till they fell apart. I still have some hats.

It was beginning to sink in that I would never have Tony with me again; to consult, appreciate, sort things out, reassure and love.

Anna was longing to explore our great city. We tried to devise a treat every day, for Anna and to help me with my strange, sad, new status of widowhood. 'What's the plan for today, Di?' she asked. She was getting restless; she was an early riser, even in the wrong hemisphere. I am too, but I wanted to write for a bit first and make a list of tasks. I usually struggled to get out of the house – decisions – what to wear? Should we visit Somerset House to see the Chelsea Arts Fair or meet my old friend Rae in Greenwich? Time for both?

Between admin and sorting, Anna and I did nice London touristy things and met friends. I was a wee bit worried the day she

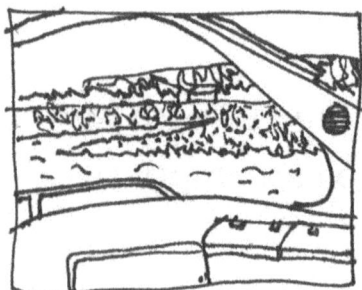

R YAR ~ Sea Pearl 29-7-06

K Sea Pearl

Teignmouth
Aug 06

ventured out on her own with an ambitious schedule: to visit the V&A, aiming for the fourth floor of ceramics and glass, as she was a superb ceramicist herself; to explore the Silver Vaults in Chancery Lane, because she collected silver treasures; and have a wander round Sloane Square, enjoying the architecture and shops. But she'd got the hang of the Tube, (the London Underground) and managed the lot successfully.

Several times during Tony's illness, our friend Kay came from the Isle of Wight to Hammersmith Hospital to sit with Tony, helping him while away the tedium of waiting around. It made a long day for her. She was one of many people who had gone out of their way to be kind. At the funeral, she and her husband had invited Anna and me, and other available family members to visit their beautiful home beneath Tennyson Down. Anna and I caught the train to Lymington and met Paul at the ferry port. Rob and Kay took us all out on the Solent in their fancy RIB, and Rob handed the controls to Paul, who gleefully roared past the Needles, those chalky rock formations looking like giant's teeth sticking out of the sea. He was thrilled, you never saw such delight on the face of a bereaved person – liberation writ large! We were only sorry that Richie missed out, because of work. We knew Tony would have loved it as he'd had that treat before. Anna made new friends and was delighted with her outing away from London.

I hoped Tony would be happy to see me spreading my wings a little. They were a bit stiff from being folded so long. *I'm sure you are delighted my lovely Tone, with this feeling of liberation after my servitude to your needs. Which I did with a happy heart, most of the time, except occasionally when I was so tired I could barely stand. But I know you forgave me. We forgave each other our transgressions.*

All too soon it was time for me to go back to work, and for Anna to head for Heathrow, back to Queensland. I wasn't keen on saying goodbye to anyone else I loved. It was a wrench parting with big sis.

The next day I returned to work, and everyone was kind. I tried to catch up, caught out by emotion now and then. But I managed to get through the day, cycled home and locked up my bike. The front door loomed. I didn't want to open it.

When I did, his absence was absolute. The silence had weight.

The Parson and his clerk
Holcombe Aug 06

Cormorant on 'The Parson'
Aug 06

44

London 2007 Tony's legacy

Dianne

You can't escape the grief, it's just to be lived through, sucked up. Maybe trawling the past and writing about it is part of mine, to reconjure him. One of the saddest parts of loss is forgetting.

This was in my notebook after he died, it looks like an apologetic prayer to Tony. It's difficult to avoid religious connotations in the word 'prayer'. Is there a substitute? Entreaty? Earnest submission?

'Sorry I teased you about our age difference all our married life, and sorry about when I was impatient and unwilling to listen. Sorry that I didn't always accept you as you were. Thank you for your great love. For always loving me so generously. Sorry, it took until you were ill for me to be totally tender towards you. Sorry about my resistance to that. But I loved you – love you – so much and you were so brave during your rotten illness. I'm glad that you are no longer suffering.

I ask for your blessing to enable me to approach life joyously, confidently, and wholeheartedly on my own and with family and friends.'

From my sculptor friend Elle, I commissioned a wood carving to remind me of our love, wherever I was.

I don't want Tony to be forgotten, because he was fabulous; a bit of a mess sometimes, like all of us. He lived through all those challenging life events, recovering from the blows and starting again, facing the next challenge and the next with vitality and enthusiasm.

I believe there's a pilot light in anyone with an addictive personality, and in troubling circumstances, it may whoosh into a conflagration. Tony's *was* ignited *and* whooshed. But help was there for the asking. The fire brigades were Gamblers Anonymous and Gam-Anon.

Since leaving Oz I've relied on friends made along the way for life support. It was easy for both of us to embrace the self-help fellowships as they were naturally a diverse community of individuals who were open and honest about their struggles. Tony and Bob's businesses had that inclusive, friendly feeling; Bob says that quite a few of the original staff members still meet up. The Community Centre in Shepherds Bush was a microcosm of a kinder world, and our wonderful friends and family were there for us, making the worst bearable, and the best brilliant.

We understood the hard way that people need people – but being part of those fellowships was purely life-enhancing. We felt lucky in the best sense, having learned to appreciate each day as we lived it. If you've suffered, you kick up your heels when the music starts.

Friends helped Tony to stop gambling and to Stay Stopped. He became an inspirational role model who influenced hundreds, perhaps thousands, of lives for the good, no matter what difficulties were happening within his own.

He made us all feel loved, and we loved him. And love is all that matters.

End

Acknowledgements

Much of the theme of this book revolves around how we were helped on the road to recovery by the kindness of friends, so it seems appropriately wonderful that the book emerges into the light because of the generosity of my eighty Kickstarter crowdfunding supporters whose names are listed at the back. Thank you all so much.

A book is a joint enterprise – the writer produces the raw material and many people help to knock it into shape. I want to thank them all for their generous gifts of time and patience, and for their sharp eyes.

Lynn, Jonny, Paul, and Jac from our writing group – thanks for your gift of close listening and gentle but incisive critiquing.

Rohan, Frances, Ellie, Elona, Ben, Kamila, Ruth and Gisèle, my early readers with constructive suggestions.

Fiona, Jill C, Isobel and Jill, members of Gam-Anon, Brian and Dr Samantha Duggan for their time and useful feedback.

Angela, Gam-Anon UK Secretary for her helpful communication.

Ben and Becky for patient reading and editorial help.

David Daniels for the cover design and encouraging pep talks.

Jane Shergold for her help and the name 'Flutter' which I initially resisted!

Tina from the delightful Hunting Raven Bookshop in Frome for her advice, support and encouragement.

Gill, Brenda and the team from Silver Crow Books for editorial help and Gill's brilliant help towards preparation for crowdfunding.

Tara Winona for making the website to support the book, www.diannesangster.com

Kat Macaulay for her time and filmmaking expertise, kickstarting the video for crowdfunding.

Douglas, Frances and Josephine from The Self Publishing Partnership for enabling it to happen.

And thanks to my amazing family for their love and support.

Supporters

The book would not have taken flight without these generous souls. I owe its existence to these people who supported me with pledges for my Kickstarter crowdfunding bid and with post-sharing. Thank you all so much.

A Mckeown
Alicja Jegor
Allinda
Ally, Tom, Theo, Osian and Vaila
Amy, Jonathan, Chloe, Sebastian and Robin
Angela Edmonds
Ann Jermain
Ann Phillips
Becky Dick and Toby Daniel
Ben Preston
Caiti Williamson
Carla Preston
Caro Elms
Catherine Francis
Catherine and Richard
Celine Thomas
Che Macolino
Cheryl Lim and Nick Greenwood

Dave, Angela, Lyla and Eloise Kaye
Diana Maynard
Eleanor Talbot
Elena Noe
Ester van Zwanenberg
George and Diana Nelson
Georgina Elms
Gilly Strong
Glynis Edwards
Gordon Alexander
Helen McCann-O'Leary
Hiwot Araya
Jac Forsyth
Jane
Janet Fizz-Curtis
Jennifer Kyte
Jill Springett
Jonny Griffiths
Judy Hosegood
June Calvert